Letter to Faculty and Students

We are pleased to offer you this collection of contemporary readings in psychology from our sister publication, *Scientific American*. In selecting articles for this anthology, we had several goals in mind. First, we tried to assemble a series of readings that would reflect something of the enormous range of topics that are being investigated in different areas of psychology today. We also looked for articles that described exciting new developments in the field. By exposing students to psychologists and other scientists describing their research and discoveries in their own words, we hope to convey the excitement of the scientific process, especially in psychology.

These articles were also chosen for their interest value and accessibility to the average college student. Such topics as the importance of sleep, the nature of intelligence and success, and how to determine if someone is lying have all been featured on mainstream news programs and television specials. Thus, these articles take you and your students to the story behind the news headlines. You'll have the opportunity to hear leading researchers not only explain their findings but also describe how the scientific process really works.

Finally, we tried to put together a group of articles that would complement the coverage in our two textbooks: *Psychology* and *Discovering Psychology*. The brief introductions at the front of this collection, written by Jason Spiegelman, provide a context for the research presented in each article and a brief overview of the article's themes. "Questions to consider" are provided to help students focus on the most salient information in the selection. They can also be used for essay assignments or to spark classroom discussion.

We hope that you and your students enjoy reading this collection. For our part, we are excited to be able to provide this snapshot of contemporary psychological research from the pages of one of America's most prestigious publications, *Scientific American*.

Don Hockenbury   **Sandy Hockenbury**

Table of

Contents

© Josee Masse

© Ken Orvidas

Magic and the Brain

Susana Martinez-Conde and Stephen L. Macknik

"Pick a card, any card!" So goes the classic introduction to the amateur illusionist's attempt to baffle, befuddle and bemuse an audience. Try though you might to undermine the magician's ability to accurately predict your card 30 or 60 seconds from now, you probably already know that you are going to find yourself completely amazed at the "magic" you are about to witness.

Audiences of magic would scarcely recognize the neurologic principles that are used to create the illusions that we find so entertaining. The sensory and perceptual systems can be manipulated to such an extent that we are sure we saw things that never happened, or, swear that something that appeared right in front of our eyes had never occurred. Cognitive principles related to attention – change blindness, inattentional blindness and choice blindness – are some of the processes that distort our perception of our surroundings.

Illusionists, particularly the most popular and successful illusionists, are able to take advantage of distractions in attention. Sometimes the cues they use to shift your focus are so subtle that they are perceived at a barely conscious level. This lack of awareness of how you have been manipulated is what makes the illusion all the more entertaining; the appearance of magic that you know cannot exist is what is so enthralling.

How is the brain involved? A rudimentary understanding of how neurons function can help explain how complex illusions can be so convincing. Page 21 gives three examples of common illusions, along with the neurophysiologic explanation for what makes these illusions so "magical." Using specific kinds of motion – straight quick movements versus long arcs through space – also cause distinctly different responses in the final location of a viewer's attention, though the exact neurologic reason for this distinction is not yet understood.

The manipulation of our perceptions, whether engaging a cause and effect fallacy, using misdirection and distraction or directing our attention in ways that are outside of our immediate awareness, lies at the heart of the illusionist's craft. After you've read this piece, you might try hard to forget your newfound knowledge so that you can fully enjoy your next trip to a magic show!

Questions to consider:

1. Do you think that our enjoyment of magic is based on our desire to believe in things that we know do not exist? Is suspension of disbelief critical to the ability to enjoy a magic show?

2. How do you think that a thorough understanding of the concepts of directed (and misdirected) attention can help us in the world of psychotherapy?

3. Some types of magic seem so obvious that you could kick yourself for not seeing the solution without an explanation. Why do you think this happens? Do we intentionally deceive ourselves as part of the "enjoyment" of the show? Is this the same as inattentional bias?

4. Do you think that knowing the neurophysiologic mechanics at play in an illusionist's act would prevent you from being deceived the next time you see such a show? If you can still be manipulated by an illusionist even if you know what is happening, then does our understanding of these mechanisms really serve any useful purpose?

Quiet! Sleeping Brain At Work

Robert Stickgold and Jeffrey M. Ellenbogen

If you are reading this collection of articles, chances are that all of the following are true: (1) you are an undergraduate college student; (2) you are taking a psychology class (probably Introduction to Psychology); and (3) you are tired. To clarify this third point, if you are an average undergraduate college student, you are probably mildly to moderately sleep deprived, having shifted your sleep schedule to meet all of your academic, social, and perhaps work-related demands. You may also engage in the regular practice of shorting yourself of sleep to do some last-minute cramming for an important exam, or even pull the occasional "all nighter" to maximize your study time.

The article by Robert Stickgold and Jeffrey Ellenbogen discusses the importance of sleep relative to cognitive skills such as memory, information retention, dreaming, performance (academic or occupational) and problem-solving. They review the history of varying beliefs regarding sleep, from the pre-1950s era when most experts believed the brain to be in a dormant "shut down" state, to the startling recognition that brain waves not only continue during sleep, but that they fluctuate regularly throughout the night. The discovery of REM and NREM stages of sleep, as well as their associated differences in brain activity, served both to answer and create many questions about the nature of human sleep.

The impact of sleep on the consolidation and solidification of memories is discussed, as well as various explanations for why sleep helps ward off the effects of interference. The relationship of both REM and slow-wave sleep stages (in fact, all stages of sleep) to increased performance of both simple and complex tasks is also outlined, as are the similarities between the brain activity of a person who is sleeping and one who is encoding long-term memories. This suggests to researchers that while we sleep we are actually practicing memories from our waking hours, thus providing more evidence that sleep is essential to memory.

Research is presented that suggests that our brains not only learn while we are asleep, perhaps by revisiting information that was experienced during our waking hours, but also continue to attempt to solve problems from our waking lives. Have you ever struggled to solve a problem while awake, only to "sleep on it" and find the solution very rapidly the next day?

The article concludes with a discussion of various theories regarding our need to sleep, discussed both in terms of evolutionary adaptation and in terms of our changing needs in a changing world.

Questions to consider:

1. Do you get enough sleep? If not, do you blame "not having enough time?" How do you think you could manage to get the 8 hours per night that is recommended for human beings? Would this be possible if you simply reconsidered your priorities?

2. Do you pay attention to your own dreams? Why or why not? Can you think of a particular dream that you've had at some point in your life that seemed very strange but that stuck with you over time?

3. Some people, called nonsomniacs, are able to exist on as few as 2 or 3 hours of sleep per night. These individuals seem to function very well with significantly less sleep than the rest of us. If you had this gift (or curse, depending on your perspective) what do you think you would do with the 4-6 hours of awake time you would gain?

4. If an individual with sleep difficulties takes a sleep-aid that (a) helps her fall asleep but (b) distorts her brain activity so that she does not experience the normal progression of sleep stages, do you think she would still feel rested the next day? Do you think she would still dream? How might her dreams be impacted by these changes?

The Secret to Raising Smart Kids

Carol S. Dweck

Stanford University psychology professor Carol S. Dweck investigates the factors that are most likely to result in a child being a high achiever in school and in life. Interestingly, she has found that innate ability (intelligence) is not the best predictor of such success, and in fact can actually hinder a child. Children who believe themselves to be naturally smart or intellectually gifted may demonstrate reduced academic effort, less resilience in the face of challenge or failure and a loss of academic motivation. To this end, Dweck advises parents not to overly praise a child's natural abilities, but to focus instead on the value of effort.

In exploring how people respond to failure, work that was inspired by Martin Seligman's study of learned helplessness, Dweck has found that our response to failure is as important as the cause of the failure itself. Those who remain positive and view failure as a challenge are more likely to overcome, while those who see failure as a personal indication of reduced value are likely to be surrender. As the Greek philosopher Epictetus said, "It's not what happens to you, but how you react to it that matters."

Dweck suggests that the responses we have to such situations depend on our views of intelligence. Those who think intelligence is fixed (helpless mindset) are unlikely to see failure as a challenge, while those who see intelligence as a skill set to be developed (growth mindset) view failure as an opportunity for growth and development.

Research presented in this article suggests that students with a growth mindset are more likely to admit when they don't know an answer and are more willing to admit their mistakes. Such students are more likely to seek out extra (or remedial) assistance when a skill set is found to be deficient because they value the process of learning more than the appearance of nonexistent skill. In the workplace, they are more likely to solicit feedback from employees and to see themselves as being a "work in progress." And, in relationships, a growth mindset can improve problem-solving.

Dweck notes that such findings do not mean that children should not be praised for success, but rather that praising the process of achieving success (the effort) is far more effective than praising the outcome (the success itself). Dweck found that students praised for their intelligence were more likely to develop a fixed mindset, while those praised for their effort developed a more growth-oriented mindset. Dweck provides advice for parents, too, with suggestions as to how they can cultivate a growth mindset in their children. Finally, Dweck describes the results of an intriguing new program that teaches students about how learning changes the brain and which encourages them to see themselves as "agents of their own brain development."

Questions to consider:

1. Do you consider intelligence to be a static or dynamic human attribute? How might fixed and growth mindsets affect success in school? In the workplace?

2. The movement to praise effort instead of outcome is not a new one. You've probably heard "it's not whether you win or lose, it's how you play the game." Do you agree with this cliché, or is the win or loss the more important factor to consider? Perhaps it is not just one or the other. What do you think?

3. How do you deal with failure, and what were you encouraged to do with failure as a child? If you are resilient and view failure as a challenge and an opportunity, why do you think others view failure as a catastrophe that requires one to give up?

4. Do you think that those who have developed a "fixed mindset" can learn to shift to a "growth mindset?" If so, how?

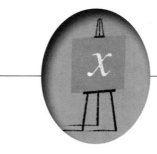

When Words Decide

Barry Schwartz

"Used" versus "preowned," "war" versus "conflict," "extended warranty" versus "service plan." Your freedom to make the choices that impact your own life is something that you may simply assume exists. Whether you are choosing a restaurant to visit for lunch, a political candidate to support or a work policy to throw your weight behind, do you always realize the various implications of the options you are being offered? Is it possible that our "free" choices are, in fact, being manipulated?

Barry Schwartz, in his article "When Words Decide," presents a compelling review of classic and modern research demonstrating that the options selected by individuals in seemingly "free choice" situations are, in fact, subject to influence based on the wording of the options presented to them. Reviewing the work of Kahneman and Tversky, Schwartz describes the manner in which those surveyed will alter their decisions when they are presented with a "gain" situation versus a "loss" situation. It seems that people are far less willing to accept risk in an option if it means sacrificing a sure gain, while they are far more willing to accept precisely the same risk if it is framed as the avoidance of a "loss." The impact of such findings can be as trivial as selecting a new pair of shoes, or as crucial as opting for a retirement savings plan that can impact your standard of living when you leave the workforce.

Schwartz also presents the concept of "prospect theory," which distinguishes a curvilinear relationship between gains and the satisfaction they bring, as well as losses and the dissatisfaction they cause. Two findings based on prospect theory are particularly interesting. First, people do not experience greater happiness based on greater achievement of positive outcomes. Instead, as positive outcomes increase, happiness and satisfaction seems to hit an upper limit. Second, people seem to have a greater capacity for feeling unhappy in response to bad outcomes than they do to feeling happy in response to positive outcomes. Does this suggest that human beings are somehow naturally "wired" to experience unhappiness and misery more readily, profoundly and automatically than happiness and satisfaction? If, in fact, this tendency describes an accurate state of affairs, what explains the human tendency to experience sorrow with greater depth and presence than joy?

Schwartz's humor and clarity makes this piece easily understood, and gives the reader an opportunity to apply salient research to his or her own experiences. Now consider the following: If this paragraph had started by discussing Schwartz's review of advanced statistics and research methodology instead of "humor and clarity," would you be more or less likely to enjoy the article?

Questions to consider:

1. Are you more likely to purchase a sale item at a store if it is advertised at "50% off when you buy two" or if it is advertised at "buy one get one free?" Do the findings from Kahneman and Tversky's research explain your preference?

2. One of the reasons why the gambling industry is so lucrative (for the industry, not for the individual player) is because people often have difficulty appreciating what they have won, instead opting to focus on what they have not yet won. How might this affect a gambler's willingness to walk away from a table when she or he is winning, even if the winnings are not very large?

3. Schwartz discusses the idea that people often tend to opt for default options, particularly when those options require no action. It is possible that this is a function of laziness, but Schwartz also suggests that people assume that "default" options are the best options. Can you think of examples where the default choices would or would not be the best choices?

4. Can you think of any examples in your life where you have "manipulated words" to elicit a choice that was in your own best interest from another person?

A Look Tells All

Siri Schubert

Have you ever been given a compliment that you felt was not genuine? Perhaps you've been told that a job interview went "very well," and yet you left with a sense that the job was going to the "other guy." How is it that we seem to know instinctively when people are not being genuine with us? According to the research of psychologist Paul Ekman, it's all in the face.

Journalist Siri Schubert interviews Paul Ekman and reviews his 40-year career studying the facial expressions that underlie basic human emotions – fear, happiness and anger, among others. Ekman notes that while we may have a natural ability to read subtle facial indications of emotional states, called microexpressions, we have to be wary of our own fallibility in this regard.

Ekman has spent a career uncovering evidence that supports the initial work of Charles Darwin, suggesting the existence of universal emotional expressions, and has demonstrated that facial expressions of emotion transcend culture. These findings were not limited to developed or "civilized" cultures. Ekman has found the same facial expressions in isolated tribal populations with minimal exposure to "modern" cultures.

The existence of microexpressions, miniscule and ephemeral changes in the musculature of the face, allows a well-trained and highly perceptive individual to sense the emotional status of another. Ekman notes, however, that is not a "mind reading" technique. While it is possible to read another's emotions, this does not give any information about the reason for the particular emotion. In other words, fear can be read in a person's face, but why the individual is afraid must be revealed in other ways.

In this article, some keys to understanding when people are giving misinformation are reviewed, including a roadmap of the facial muscles and the types of questioning strategies that can be used to reveal an individual's intent to deceive. Ekman also warns about making "Othello's Error," which leaves us overly confident and certain of our ability to read expressions. There are many indications of an emotional state, and facial expressions are one of many to which an individual must attend.

Questions to consider:

1. Are you a good liar? Would your friends or family be able to tell if you were lying? How so?

2. Can you think of some situations where being an expert reader of microexpressions could give you an advantage over other people?

3. If facial expressions of emotion are indeed ubiquitous across cultures, why do we still seem to have difficulty reading the intentions of those from countries or cultures different than our own?

4. If you could choose one emotion to be able to read with perfect accuracy in others, what would it be and why?

Why It's So Hard To Be Happy

Michael Wiederman

Is happiness founded in the accumulation of possessions? Do we experience greater contentment with life if we have the perfect job, the perfect house, the perfect partner? Research into the human experience of happiness is the topic of this discussion by psychologist Michael Wiederman.

While many people convince themselves that their lot in life would be better if they had greater financial means, research has not supported this concept. Wealth and financial security as measured by "buying power" has increased threefold since 1950, but survey research has found that happiness has not increased at the same pace; in fact, happiness does not seem to have increased at all! In fact, anxiety has risen in a linear fashion, poking holes in the notion that money can buy happiness.

Evolutionary theory suggests that attending more to the negative factors or changes in our environment was an adaptive human tendency, and thus we may have "inherited" a resistance to experiencing happiness and a hypersensitivity to dissatisfaction. The outcome of thousands of generations of evolution may be seen in personality tendencies today, which have been found to have a strong genetic component.

Genetics are not enough to explain happiness, however, as there is a very salient contribution of both environmental contributions and individual behaviors. One might, therefore, assume that our own actions, efforts and realization of personal goals would be satisfactory for achieving personal happiness. Right? Unfortunately, research also finds that this is not the case. Social comparison seems to be the reason why this path to happiness leads to a dead end, as we are not content simply with our own accomplishments; instead, we seem to evaluate our own lot in life relative to the situations and accomplishments of others. This tendency of trying to "keep up with the Joneses" is another ingredient in the complex recipe that helps cook dissatisfaction rather than happiness.

In a very real way, the lack of happiness that results from the accruing of material possessions is similar to the lack of happiness that comes from the achievement of goals. The issue is that happiness is not found in the "having," but rather in the "getting." Mihaly Csikszentmihalyi's work describing the concept of positive "flow" has been a step forward in the understanding of happiness. However, as long as we set our sights on the destination and not the journey, we will be unable to become immersed in the process. The overriding message of happiness research is that if we stay destination-focused, we will miss the entire trip!

Questions to consider:

1. How do you define happiness in your life? Are you a generally happy person or a generally unhappy person? Do you think your current level of happiness is a result of your personality and attitude toward life or of your outward circumstances and environment?

2. How have you selected an academic major or a career path? What criteria have been most important in your decision - personal fulfillment and satisfaction or financial security? Do you think money can buy you happiness? Why or why not?

3. Research into happiness suggests that you should be fully in the moment, focusing on now instead of looking too much to the future. Other research suggests that taking immediate rewards is often a poor choice, as delay of gratification can make the reward much more valuable. How do you think these two seemingly incompatible concepts can be reconciled?

4. The article discusses the pursuit of happiness in the context of research in the United States. Do you think that people in other cultures might view happiness differently? How might the individualistic emphasis of the U.S. affect beliefs about happiness? Is happiness something that we are taught to experience in different ways in different cultures?

5. Consider the author's six suggestions for increasing happiness. Do you agree with all six suggestions? How could you implement these strategies in your own life?

Big Answers from Little People

David Dobbs

Are we born with instinctive levels of knowledge, or do we come into the world a blank slate? Philosophers and psychologists alike have pondered this issue for centuries, but Harvard University psychologist Elizabeth Spelke is seeking some actual answers. Author David Dobbs' profile of Dr. Spelke and her research presents us with some compelling information about the abilities of infants who are not yet able to crawl or talk. Spelke's findings may drastically alter our conception of adult cognition.

Using techniques first introduced by Robert Fantz in the 1950s, Spelke studied how much time infants spent looking at various types of stimuli, and found that they demonstrate recognition of the connection between visual and auditory stimuli based on their length of gaze. She has also been able to make distinctions between a baby's ability to recognize quantity differences, interpret when illogical interruptions of motion have occurred, and predict which object out of two an adult will grab based on that adult's gaze. Such findings have collectively been used to suggest that children are born with an existing set of cognitive schema, and the process of adjusting and adapting to information from their new surroundings may be as salient as the need to acquire novel schemas. This "set" of preexisting information is what Spelke refers to as "core knowledge."

Spelke's model, which is referred to by some as a "nativist" position, is shared by other noted researchers, including linguist Noam Chomsky. Chomsky's theories claim that children are born with the basic essentials needed to acquire and use language skills.

Spelke was quite vocal, although civil, in her response to public statements by Lawrence Summer, who was president of Harvard University at the time, that biological factors helped explain the low number of female math and science professors. She has argued that all of the evidence suggests that we are born with no basic distinctions in our cognitive abilities, and that an equal playing field designed to stimulate such abilities would surely lead to equal development of those skills into adulthood. Her cogent and eloquent arguments led to the establishment of a $50 million fund designed to support female and minority faculty at Harvard University.

Questions to consider:

1. What do you think of the assumption held by many that men are biologically prewired to be better at certain cognitive skills while women are biologically prewired to be better at others? Do you think this assumption has any validity, and if so how are these differences adaptive or maladaptive to humanity?

2. The foundation of Spelke's conclusions comes from a child's willingness and ability to gaze at certain visual stimuli for longer than other stimuli. What do you think of drawing such wide-reaching conclusions from such limited behavior differences?

3. What do you think about the nature of children's cognitive skills at birth? Are you of the "children are born as a blank slate" school of thought, or are you more along the lines of a nativist? Perhaps you fall somewhere in between! Has your view changed after reading this piece?

Set in Our Ways

Nikolas Westerhoff

Do people accuse you of being "in a rut" or unwilling to try new things? Conversely, does it bother you when friends seem to be less open to new experiences than they used to be? Psychologist and science journalist Nikolas Westerhoff presents compelling research into personality theories that describe a tendency to lose our spontaneity, adventurousness and openness to new experiences as we age, and he offers some explanations as to why these age-related trends appear across different cultures and populations. These explanations also neatly explain why this tendency toward openness, while declining after our 20s, tends to re-emerge in our late years, typically after the age of 60.

This piece reviews the theory of the Five Factor model ("The Big Five") of personality, which includes the five "supertraits" of openness to new experiences, conscientiousness, extroversion, agreeableness and neuroticism (conveniently remembered using the acronym "OCEAN"). Data gleaned from thousands of research participants have found that the first factor – openness – predictably declines once "young adulthood" is over, and the ubiquity of this finding across cultures has prompted two different explanations.

One model suggests that the tendency to become less open as we age may be genetic, but a more likely explanation proposes that the responsibilities of adulthood explain this tendency. It may well be that adults are simply less willing to explore new avenues that offer less certainty and stability because the obligations and responsibilities of adulthood extend beyond themselves. The reduction in the immediacy of these obligations near retirement age – a reduction that indeed permits retirement to occur – may explain why openness begins to increase again in our later years.

Sociologist Deborah Carr also finds that that even negative life events – death of a loved one, loss of a job, realization of a disease – can stimulate effective life change that would have been resisted without the negative event. If you've ever listened to the lyrics of Tim McGraw's song "Live Like You Were Dying," the basis of Carr's theory would be very clear.

Questions to consider:

1. What changes do you want to make in your life, and what prevents you from making those changes? Do you think your age has anything to do with it? Have you noticed that your willingness to engage in new, unfamiliar activities has decreased or increased as you have gotten older?

2. The stereotype of senior citizens eating at the same restaurant day in and day out and sticking to a solid and predictable routine does not seem to be consistent with the findings that openness increases in our later years. How would you reconcile these two bits of information?

3. Do you like to eat at the same restaurant and order the same meal? Would you prefer to vacation in a familiar location or explore somewhere new? Do you think your tendency toward openness is related to your age?

4. Many people complain about their cable or cell phone provider, but few actually switch. Why do you think that is? Do we prefer the familiar even when we dislike it over the risk of something that is potentially better yet unknown?

Freud at 150: Neurotic about Neurons

Steve Ayan

One of the most influential and simultaneously controversial figures in the entire field of psychology was, and remains, Dr. Sigmund Freud. From his early beginnings as a physician to his landmark theories regarding the nature of the human mind, his ideas catapulted the field of psychology into an entirely new way of thinking. Virtually all current theories in the field have addressed the concepts of the unconscious, psychosexual development, and the structures of the personality that were hypothesized by Freud, even if those theories have been vehement in their rejection of these concepts. Given this lengthy history and this wide-ranging influence, how are Freud's theories explored today, over 150 years after his birth?

Author Steve Ayan provides a concise yet thorough history of Freud's ascent from a humble neurologist who received his medical degree at the age of 25 to the founder of the psychoanalytic school of thought. His early work with Jean-Martin Charcot and Joseph Breuer, including training in the gentle "art" of hypnosis, is described as the path that led Freud to his belief that the hysterical symptoms of female patients were caused by unseen mechanisms. These causes, eventually dubbed "unconscious," formed the basis of Freud's lifelong work in psychoanalysis. Talk therapy, including free association, was developed as a means of uncovering (or recovering) these unconscious determinants of psychiatric symptoms, and it was not long before Freud discovered the value of dreams in analysis.

As Ayan points out, Freud's fascination with the psychological value in dream interpretation marked his total digression from the field of neurology. It also has been suggested that this is where his theories took leave of true scientific quality. He was never to find a way to reconcile the mind-body question, and it was others who discovered the basic physical components of the human brain, and, some say, the mind.

Today, the field of neuroscience has not uncovered a direct connection between the physical and the unconscious components of the human mind. There are ongoing attempts to validate the scientific basis of Freud's theories, such as the new field called "neuropsychoanalysis." However, for now, biological evidence for psychoanalytic theory remains elusive.

Questions to consider:

1. Why do you think that Freud conjures up such passionate responses in today's psychological, psychiatric, and medical communities?

2. Do you agree or disagree with Freud's basic assumptions? Do you think he was a genius or a madman? Do you fall somewhere in between?

3. Which parts of Freud's theories do you think have the most validity? Do you have any personal experiences that can verify his assertions?

The Science of Team Success

Steve W.J. Kozlowski and Daniel R. Ilgen

Are you a fan of "Survivor," "The Apprentice" or other reality show? If so, you've surely noticed that at some point in each competition, individuals are required to work effectively and efficiently as teams. Although each competitor is distinctly interested in his or her own success, unwillingness to work effectively for the success of teammates ultimately leads to a risk of individual failure.

Steve Kozlowski and Daniel Ilgen present several concepts of effective teamwork alongside a clear call to action – a call that suggests that ignoring the principles of effective teamwork and engaging in actions that, in fact, undermine effective teamwork is ultimately detrimental to outcomes. The significance of those outcomes depends, of course, on the project at hand, but they can range from a grade on a classroom group assignment to the life and death circumstances of disasters like Hurricane Katrina or the Indonesia Tsunami.

There are several factors to consider when evaluating the potential effectiveness of a team. Is a team really needed, or is the task at hand one that is more easily and effectively accomplished with individual effort? If a team is needed, what kind of team will be the most likely to produce positive outcomes? Is face-to-face communication required for greatest productivity? Can virtual conferencing, such as web meetings, adequately substitute for face-to-face interactions? What is the effect of team members leaving and being replaced by others, even if the new member has all of the requisite knowledge to serve as an effective proxy?

Additional questions of a more interpersonal nature include the following: What happens when team leadership is not effectively administered? Do team members' moods and attitudes influence the team's productivity, and if so, how? Is team productivity enhanced when team members take time to socialize outside of their work-related tasks and enjoy each other as "friends" rather than "colleagues?" What concrete strategies can team leaders adopt to increase the likelihood of team success?

Consider these questions and look for some research-based answers as you enjoy this article. Consider these data the next time you are assigned a group project in a class. Think about how you can ensure positive and effective teamwork even before the topic of the assignment is addressed.

Questions to consider:

1. Are the facets of teamwork discussed in the article the same in cultures that place a premium on individualism as in those cultures that value collectivism?

2. Is it always counterproductive to reward individual effort in a team setting? Can such rewards actually motivate a team, or will they always lead to resentment and jealousy, emotions that can hinder team progress?

3. Is the need to achieve individual success always at odds with the need to achieve team success? Is individual success somehow diminished or muted if it must be shared with a team?

4. Let's say you were a professional baseball player. You have a choice of winning a World Series as a team or winning the MVP (Most Valuable Player) award for the entire league. You can only have one or the other. Which would you choose, and why? Would your answer be different if one accolade brought more personal financial reward? Do you think professional athletes who play on a team have lost their team mentality to the detriment of the overall sport? Why or why not?

5. How do you think one can effectively deal with a team leader who is not doing his or her job properly? Should that person use the same interventions with a team member who is not pulling their weight?

Cure in the Mind

Maj-Britt Niemi

Do you have friends or relatives who swear that they regained their health after experiencing an unconventional healing method or using a treatment that is not accepted in mainstream medicine? Do you know of anyone who experienced a "miraculous" recovery from an illness or injury that physicians claimed could not be treated?

One common explanation of such unexplained cures is "placebo effect." But what exactly is the placebo effect? How does it work?

A *placebo* is a sham or fake treatment. In this fascinating article, psychologist Maj-Britt Niemi describes the history of research into the placebo effect and details some of the mechanisms through which fake treatments might produce real cures. These mechanisms include *non-conscious* conditioned responses to a particular drug or treatment and *conscious* expectations that a treatment will be effective.

Placebos have been shown to be effective in illnesses ranging from cancer to Parkinson's disease and multiple sclerosis, as well as in pain. Controlled studies have shown that placebos can affect immune responses in animals as well as humans. In explaining how placebos might work, Niemi distinguishes among the different brain pathways that are probably involved in different types of placebo effects. For example, expectations are likely involved in pain control, while classical conditioning is a more likely explanation for immune system responses to placebo treatments.

Niemi notes that there are subconscious mechanisms that relate to the expectation of recovering, as well as the mental impact of actually receiving treatment. Clearly, one's belief that effective treatment (1) does exist and (2) is being received is correlated with better medical outcomes. Conversely, the belief that one is receiving treatments designed to lower physical functioning has also been shown effective, even when the treatment received was completely inert. Niemi points to research into the relationship between the placebo effect and decreased immune functioning as evidence of this fact.

Here is the real question, of course: is the expectation that we will recover from an illness enough to prompt recovery? Can placebo therapy replace true medicine? Clearly the answer to this question is "no." Medical illness, as well as the recovery from such, is not a question of "mind over matter." With that said, however, mind does matter.

Questions to consider:

1. Have you ever received a placebo treatment? Were you aware of it while you were being treated? Did your awareness of the fact that the treatment was not effective impact your recovery?

2. How might placebo treatments be very effective for someone suffering from a psychological, rather than a physical, illness?

3. If a person requires a medication but has, say, an allergy or a heightened sensitivity to the side effects of that medication, do you think a placebo can work just as well?

4. Other than the mechanisms of effect that are noted by Dr. Niemi, how else might sham treatments work? Can you think of any other explanation for the effect of placebo treatments?

Magic and the Brain

Magicians have been testing and exploiting the limits of cognition and attention for hundreds of years. Neuroscientists are just beginning to catch up

By Susana Martinez-Conde and Stephen L. Macknik

KEY CONCEPTS

■ Magic tricks often work by covert misdirection, drawing the spectator's attention away from the secret "method" that makes a trick work.

■ Neuroscientists are scrutinizing magic tricks to learn how they can be put to work in experimental studies that probe aspects of consciousness not necessarily grounded in current sensory reality.

■ Brain imaging shows that some regions are particularly active during certain kinds of magic tricks.

—*The Editors*

The spotlight shines on the magician's assistant. The woman in the tiny white dress is a luminous beacon of beauty radiating from the stage to the audience. The Great Tomsoni announces he will change her dress from white to red. On the edge of their seats, the spectators strain to focus on the woman, burning her image deep into their retinas. Tomsoni claps his hands, and the spotlight dims ever so briefly before reflaring in a blaze of red. The woman is awash in a flood of redness.

Whoa, just a moment there! Switching color with the spotlight is not exactly what the audience had in mind. The magician stands at the side of the stage, looking pleased at his little joke. Yes, he admits, it was a cheap trick; his favorite kind, he explains devilishly. But you have to agree, he did turn her dress red—along with the rest of her. Please, indulge him and direct your attention once more to his beautiful assistant as he switches the lights back on for the next trick. He claps his hands, and the lights dim again; then the stage explodes in a supernova of whiteness. But wait! Her dress really has turned red. The Great Tomsoni has done it again!

The trick and its explanation by John Thompson (aka the Great Tomsoni) reveal a deep intuitive understanding of the neural processes taking place in the spectators' brains—the kind of understanding that we neuroscientists can appropriate for our own scientific benefit. Here's how

the trick works. As Thompson introduces his assistant, her skintight white dress wordlessly lures the spectators into assuming that nothing—certainly not another dress—could possibly be hiding under the white one. That reasonable assumption, of course, is wrong. The attractive woman in her tight dress also helps to focus people's attention right where Thompson wants it— on the woman's body. The more they stare at her, the less they notice the hidden devices in the floor, and the better adapted their retinal neurons become to the brightness of the light and the color they perceive.

All during Thompson's patter after his little "joke," each spectator's visual system is undergoing a brain process called neural adaptation. The responsiveness of a neural system to a constant stimulus (as measured by the firing rate of the relevant neurons) decreases with time. It is as if neurons actively ignore a constant stimulus to save their strength for signaling that a stimulus is changing. When the constant stimulus is turned off, the adapted neurons fire a "rebound" response known as an afterdischarge.

In this case, the adapting stimulus is the red-lit dress, and Thompson knows that the spectators' retinal neurons will rebound for a fraction of a second after the lights are dimmed. The audience will continue to see a red afterimage in the shape of the woman. During that split second, a trap door in the stage opens briefly, and

JEAN-FRANCOIS PODEVIN (*hat and wand*); MISHA GRAVENOR (*Penn & Teller*)

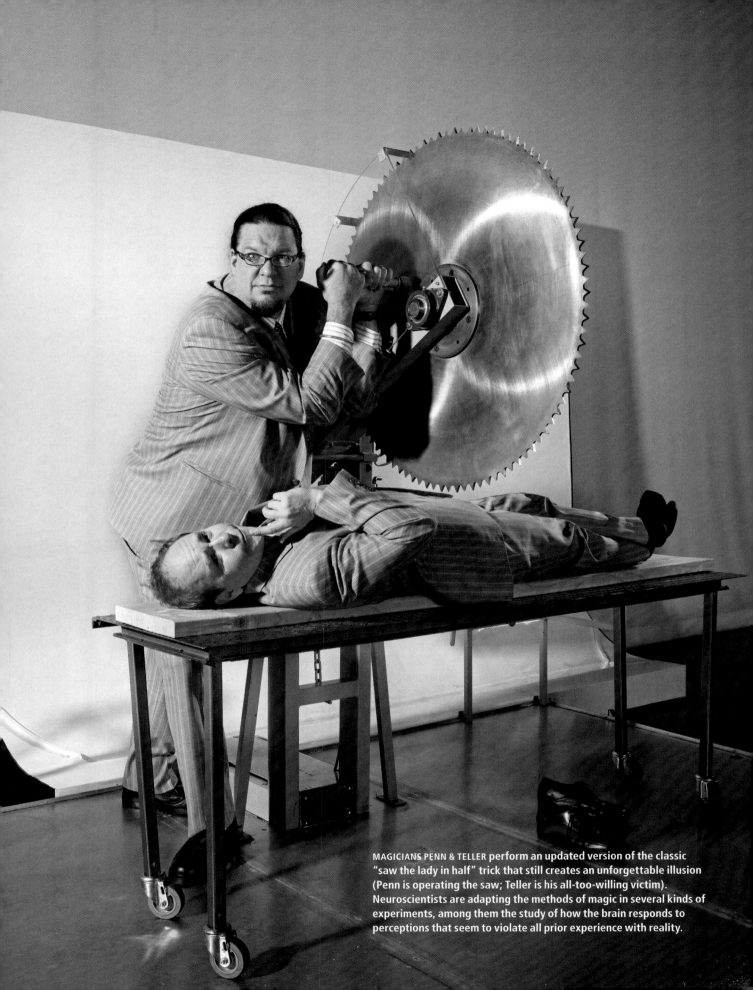

MAGICIANS PENN & TELLER perform an updated version of the classic "saw the lady in half" trick that still creates an unforgettable illusion (Penn is operating the saw; Teller is his all-too-willing victim). Neuroscientists are adapting the methods of magic in several kinds of experiments, among them the study of how the brain responds to perceptions that seem to violate all prior experience with reality.

FOOLING MIND OR EYE?

An illusion based on the painting *Enigma*, by French artist Isia Léviant, often induces a false sense of flowing movement in the concentric rings (stare at the center dot in the picture). But does the illusion originate in the mind or in the eye? The evidence was conflicting until the authors and their colleagues showed in October that the illusory motion is driven by microsaccades—small, involuntary eye movements that occur during visual fixation. Knowing the roles of eye and mind in magic is essential before the illusions of magic can be used as experimental tools in neuroscience.

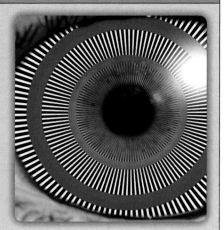

COGNITIVE ILLUSIONS

Neuroscientists are studying the ways magicians exploit mental lapses, among them:

■ **CHANGE BLINDNESS**
A viewer misses changes made to a scene during a brief interruption.

EXAMPLE: Color of furniture is changed between scenes of a play.

■ **INATTENTIONAL BLINDNESS**
A spectator does not perceive items that are plainly in view.

EXAMPLE: A person in a gorilla suit wanders into a scene and goes unnoticed.

■ **CHOICE BLINDNESS**
A spectator explains the reasons for a choice, even though the choice was not made.

EXAMPLE: A man does not notice when a photograph he selected is secretly swapped for another and explains his "preference" for the latter [see box at bottom of page 21].

■ **ILLUSORY CORRELATION**
One unrelated event appears to cause another.

EXAMPLE: A magician waves a wand, and a rabbit appears.

the white dress, held only lightly in place with Velcro and attached to invisible cables leading under the stage, is ripped from her body. Then the lights come back up.

Two other factors help to make the trick work. First, the lighting is so bright just before the dress comes off that when it dims, the spectators cannot see the rapid motions of the cables and the white dress as they disappear underneath the stage. The same temporary blindness can overtake you when you walk from a sunny street into a dimly lit shop. Second, Thompson performs the real trick only after the audience thinks it is already over. That gains him an important cognitive advantage—the spectators are not looking for a trick at the critical moment, and so they slightly relax their scrutiny.

The New Science of Neuromagic

Thompson's trick nicely illustrates the essence of stage magic. Magicians are, first and foremost, artists of attention and awareness. They manipulate the focus and intensity of human attention, controlling, at any given instant, what we are aware of and what we are not. They do so in part by employing bewildering combinations of visual illusions (such as afterimages), optical illusions (smoke and mirrors), special effects (explosions, fake gunshots, precisely timed lighting controls), sleight of hand, secret devices and mechanical artifacts ("gimmicks").

But the most versatile instrument in their bag of tricks may be the ability to create cognitive illusions. Like visual illusions, cognitive illusions mask the perception of physical reality. Yet unlike visual illusions, cognitive illusions are not sensory in nature. Rather they involve high-level

functions such as attention, memory and causal inference. With all those tools at their disposal, well-practiced magicians make it virtually impossible to follow the physics of what is actually happening—leaving the impression that the only explanation for the events is magic.

Neuroscientists are just beginning to catch up with the magician's facility in manipulating attention and cognition. Of course the aims of neuroscience are different from those of magic; the neuroscientist seeks to understand the brain and neuron underpinnings of cognitive functions, whereas the magician wants mainly to exploit cognitive weaknesses. Yet the techniques developed by magicians over centuries of stage magic could also be subtle and powerful probes in the hands of neuroscientists, supplementing and perhaps expanding the instruments already in experimental use.

Neuroscience is becoming familiar with the methods of magic by subjecting magic itself to scientific study—in some cases showing for the first time how some of its methods work in the brain. Many studies of magic conducted so far confirm what is known about cognition and attention from earlier work in experimental psychology. A cynic might dismiss such efforts: Why do yet another study that simply confirms what is already well known? But such criticism misses the importance and purpose of the studies. By investigating the techniques of magic, neuroscientists can familiarize themselves with methods that they can adapt to their own purposes. Indeed, we believe that cognitive neuroscience could have advanced faster had investigators probed magicians' intuitions earlier. Even today magicians may have a few tricks up their sleeves that neuroscientists have not yet adopted.

By applying the tools of magic, neuroscientists can hope to learn how to design more robust experiments and to create more effective cognitive and visual illusions for exploring the neural bases of attention and awareness. Such techniques could not only make experimental studies of cognition possible with clever and highly attentive subjects; they could also lead to diagnostic and treatment methods for patients suffering from specific cognitive deficits—such as attention deficits resulting from brain trauma, ADHD (attention-deficit hyperactivity disorder), Alzheimer's disease, and the like. The methods of magic might also be put to work in "tricking" patients to focus on the most important parts of their therapy, while suppressing distractions that cause confusion and disorientation.

COURTESY OF JORGE OTERO-MILLAN *Laboratory of Visual Neuroscience*

Magicians use the general term "misdirection" to refer to the practice of diverting the spectator's attention away from a secret action. In the lingo of magic, misdirection draws the audience's attention toward the "effect" and away from the "method," the secret behind the effect. Borrowing some terms from cognitive psychology, we have classified misdirection as "overt" and "covert." The misdirection is overt if the magician redirects the spectator's gaze away from the method—perhaps simply by asking the audience to look at a particular object. When the Great Tomsoni introduces his lovely assistant, for instance, he ensures that all eyes are on her.

"Covert" misdirection, in contrast, is a subtler technique; there, too, the magician draws the spectator's attentional spotlight—or focus of suspicion—away from the method, but without necessarily redirecting the spectator's gaze. Under the influence of covert misdirection, spectators may be looking directly at the method behind the trick yet be entirely unaware of it.

Cognitive neuroscience already recognizes at least two kinds of covert misdirection. In what is called change blindness, people fail to notice that something about a scene is different from the way it was before. The change may be expected or unexpected, but the key feature is that observers do not notice it by looking at the scene at any one instant in time. Instead the observer must compare the postchange state with the prechange state.

Many studies have shown that changes need not be subtle to cause change blindness. Even dramatic alterations in a visual scene go unnoticed if they take place during a transient interruption such as a blink, a saccadic eye movement (in which the eye quickly darts from one point to another) or a flicker of the scene. The "color-changing card trick" video by psychologist and magician Richard Wiseman of the University of Hertfordshire in England is a dramatic example of the phenomenon (the video is available online at www.youtube.com/watch?v=voAntzB7EwE). In Wiseman's demonstration—which you must see to appreciate—viewers fail to notice shifts in color that take place off camera. It is worth noting that despite its name, the color-changing card trick video does not use magic to make its point.

Inattentional blindness differs from change blindness in that there is no need to compare the current scene with a scene from memory. Instead people fail to notice an unexpected object that is fully visible directly in front of them. Psychologist Daniel J. Simons invented a classic example of the genre. Simons and psychologist Christopher F. Chabris, both then at Harvard University, asked observers to count how many times a "team" of three basketball players pass a ball to each other, while ignoring the passes made by three other players. While they concentrated on counting, half of the observers failed to notice

[THE AUTHORS]

Susana Martinez-Conde and Stephen L. Macknik are at the Barrow Neurological Institute in Phoenix, where Martinez-Conde is director of the Laboratory of Visual Neuroscience and Macknik is director of the Laboratory of Behavioral Neurophysiology. Their article "Windows on the Mind" appeared in the August 2007 issue of Scientific American. The authors thank their magician collaborators for sharing many insights: Mac King, James Randi (aka the Amaz!ng Randi), Apollo Robbins, Teller (from Penn & Teller) and John Thompson (aka the Great Tomsoni). They are also grateful to the Association for the Scientific Study of Consciousness and the Mind Science Foundation.

[CHANGE BLINDNESS]

CAN YOU KEEP US FROM READING YOUR MIND?

Can you explain the astounding results of the following mind-reading experiment by Clifford Pickover, a prolific author of popular books about science and mathematics? The editors of *Scientific American* have prepared a simulated Pickover test that you can take here, or you can try the even more puzzling online version at http://sprott.physics.wisc.edu/pickover/esp.html. By using his system of ESP, we think we can predict the correct outcome of your choice with 98 percent accuracy. To begin, pick one of the six cards below and remember it.

Say its name aloud several times so you won't forget it. Once you're sure you'll remember it, circle one of the eyes in the row below. Then turn to page 23.

JEFF NOBLE (Martinez-Conde and Macknik)

HOW TO PULL COINS OUT OF THIN AIR

The magician Teller relies on misdirection and sleight of hand to create an illusion called the Miser's Dream. He begins by secretly palming six coins in

each hand, then apparently produces the coins out of anything he can reach—his own hair, the clothing of his spectators, empty space—and tosses them into

Having demonstrated his bucket is empty, Teller starts producing coins in his right hand.

By directing his gaze to his right hand, he diverts his audience's attention from his left hand. But it is the left hand, the one holding the bucket, from which he is dropping hidden coins.

In fact, he is repeatedly producing the same coin in his right hand.

Just as the audience begins to suspect that Teller is simply dropping palmed coins from his right hand, he drops five of the six coins from his right hand all at once. That astounds the audience, because he could not have palmed 11 coins in his right hand.

that a person in a gorilla suit walks across the scene (the gorilla even stops briefly at the center of the scene and beats its chest!). No abrupt interruption or distraction was necessary to create this effect; the counting task was so absorbing that many observers who were looking directly at the gorilla nonetheless missed it.

Tricking the Eye or Tricking the Brain?

Magicians consider the covert form of misdirection more elegant than the overt form. But neuroscientists want to know what kinds of neural and brain mechanisms enable a trick to work. If the artistry of magic is to be adapted by neuroscience, neuroscientists must understand what kinds of cognitive processes that artistry is tapping into.

Perhaps the first study to correlate the perception of magic with a physiological measurement was published in 2005 by psychologists Gustav Kuhn of Durham University in England and Benjamin W. Tatler of the University of Dundee in Scotland. The two investigators measured the eye movements of observers while Kuhn, who is also a magician, made a cigarette "disappear" by dropping it below a table. One of their goals was to determine whether observers missed the trick because they were not looking in the right place at the right time or because they did not attend to it, no matter which direction they were

looking. The results were clear: it made no difference where they were looking.

A similar study of another magic trick, the "vanishing-ball illusion," provides further evidence that the magician is manipulating the spectators' attention at a high cognitive level; the direction of their gaze is not critical to the effect. In the vanishing-ball illusion the magician begins by tossing a ball straight up and catching it several times without incident. Then, on the final toss, he only pretends to throw the ball. His head and eyes follow the upward trajectory of an imaginary ball, but instead of tossing the ball, he secretly palms it. What most spectators perceive, however, is that the (unthrown) ball ascends—and then vanishes in midair.

The year after his study with Tatler, Kuhn and neurobiologist Michael F. Land of the University of Sussex in England discovered that the spectators' gaze did not point to where they themselves claimed to have seen the ball vanish. The finding suggested the illusion did not fool the brain systems responsible for the spectators' eye motions. Instead, Kuhn and Land concluded, the magician's head and eye movements were critical to the illusion, because they covertly redirected the spectators' attentional focus (rather than their gaze) to the predicted position of the ball. The neurons that responded to the implied motion of the ball suggested by the magician's head and eye movements are found in the same

a metal bucket with a loud clank. The deception depends in part on social cues such as head position and gaze direction.

Teller produces the final palmed coin from his right hand, then turns his hand to show that his palm is, in fact, empty.

Spectacularly, Teller throws the 11 coins from the bucket as he continues to hold the final coin in his right hand.

visual areas of the brain as neurons that are sensitive to real motion. If implied and real motion activate similar neural circuits, perhaps it is no wonder that the illusion seems so realistic.

Kuhn and Land hypothesized that the vanishing ball may be an example of "representational momentum." The final position of a moving object that disappears is perceived to be farther along its path than its actual final position—as if the predicted position was extrapolated from the motion that had just gone before.

More Tools of the Trickery Trade

Spectators often try to reconstruct magic tricks to understand what happened during the show—

after all, the more the observer tries (and fails) to understand the trick, the more it seems as if it is "magic." For their part, magicians often dare their audiences to discover their methods, say, by "proving" that a hat is empty or an assistant's dress is too tight to conceal a second dress underneath. Virtually everything done is done to make the reconstruction as hard as possible, via misdirection.

But change blindness and inattentional blindness are not the only kinds of cognitive illusions magicians can pull out of a hat. Suppose a magician needs to raise a hand to execute a trick. Teller, half of the renowned stage magic act known as Penn & Teller, explains that if he raises his hand for no apparent reason, he is more likely to draw suspicion than if he makes a hand gesture—such as adjusting his glasses or scratching his head—that seems natural or spontaneous. To magicians, such gestures are known as "informing the motion."

Unspoken assumptions and implied information are also important to both the perception of a trick and its subsequent reconstruction. Magician James Randi ("the Amaz!ng Randi") notes that spectators are more easily lulled into accepting suggestions and unspoken information than direct assertions. Hence, in the reconstruction the spectator may remember implied suggestions as if they were direct proof.

Psychologists Petter Johansson and Lars Hall, both at Lund University in Sweden, and their colleagues have applied this and other magic techniques in developing a completely novel way of addressing neuroscientific questions. They presented picture pairs of female faces to naive experimental subjects and asked the subjects to choose which face in each pair they found more attractive. On some trials the sub-

FROM NATURE REVIEWS NEUROSCIENCE, JULY 30, 2008, REPRINTED BY PERMISSION OF MACMILLAN PUBLISHERS LTD (a–d)

VISUAL ILLUSIONS IN MAGIC

Not all magic is cognitive. Exploiting well-known properties of the visual system can also lead to unusual effects, among them:

■ **SPOON BENDING**
A magician shakes a spoon, making its neck appear flexible.

WHY IT WORKS:
Neurons in the visual cortex sensitive to both motion and line endings respond differently to oscillations than other visual neurons do. The result is an apparent discrepancy between the ends of a stimulus and its center; a solid object seems to flex in the middle.

■ **THE RETENTION OF VISION VANISH**
The magician removes an object from the visual field, but it still appears visible for a short time.

WHY IT WORKS:
Neural afterdischarge produces afterimages for about 100 milliseconds after a stimulus ceases.

■ **JERRY ANDRUS'S TRIZONAL SPACE WARP**
Spectators stare at a spinning disk with three zones of expanding and contracting motion. When they then look at a stationary object, it, too, seems to expand and contract.

WHY IT WORKS:
Neurons adapt differently to the motions in the three zones of the visual field.

[CHOICE BLINDNESS]

INDUCING FALSE NARRATIVES

In an experiment, subjects were shown pairs of photographs (a) and asked to choose the more attractive image (b). After each choice, the experimenters turned the photographs face down (c) and used sleight of hand to swap some of the chosen images for the rejected ones. The "choice" was then once again turned face up, and the subjects were asked to explain their preference. Even when the choice shown was actually the rejected image (d), many subjects constructed an "explanation" for the choice. The urge for people to fit what they falsely think are their own choices into an internally consistent narrative can thus often supplant the memory of their actual selections.

jects were also asked to describe the reasons for their choice. Unknown to the subjects, the investigators occasionally used a sleight-of-hand technique, learned from a professional magician named Peter Rosengren, to switch one face for the other—*after* the subjects made their choice. Thus, for the pairs that were secretly manipulated, the result of the subject's choice became the opposite of his or her initial intention.

Intriguingly, the subjects noticed the switch in only 26 percent of all the manipulated pairs. But even more surprising, when the subjects were asked to state the reasons for their choice in a manipulated trial, they confabulated to justify the outcome—an outcome that was the opposite of their actual choice! Johansson and his colleagues call the phenomenon "choice blindness." By tacitly but strongly suggesting the subjects had already made a choice, the investigators were able to study how people justify their choices—even choices they do not actually make.

The Pickpocket Who Picks Your Brain

Misdirection techniques might also be developed out of the skills of the pickpocket. Such thieves, who often ply their trade in dense public spaces, rely heavily on socially based misdirection—gaze contact, body contact and invasion of the personal space of the victim, or "mark." Pickpockets may also move their hands in distinct ways, depending on their present purpose. They may sweep out a curved path if they want to attract the mark's attention to the entire path of motion, or they may trace a fast, linear path if they want to reduce attention to the path and quickly shift the mark's attention to the final position. The neuroscientific underpinnings of these maneuvers are unknown, but our research collaborator Apollo Robbins, a professional pickpocket, has emphasized that the two kinds of motions are essential to effectively misdirecting the mark. We have proposed several possible, testable explanations.

One proposal is that curved and straight hand motions activate two distinct control systems in the brain for moving the eyes. The "pursuit" system controls the eyes when they follow smoothly moving objects, whereas the "saccadic" system controls movements in which the eyes jump from one visual target to the next. So we have hypothesized that the pickpocket's curved hand motions may trigger eye control by the mark's pursuit system, whereas fast, straight motions may cause the saccadic system to take the lead. Then if the mark's pursuit system locks onto the curved trajectory of the pickpocket's hand, the center of the mark's vision may be drawn away from the location of a hidden theft. And if fast, straight motions engage the mark's saccadic system, the pickpocket gains the advantage that the mark's vision is suppressed while the eye darts from point to point. (The phenomenon is well known in the vision sciences as saccadic suppression.)

Another possible explanation for the distinct hand motions is that curved motions may be perceptually more salient than linear ones and hence attract stronger attention. If so, only the attentional system of the brain—not any control system for eye motions—may be affected by the pickpocket's manual misdirection. Our earlier studies have shown that the curves and corners of objects are more salient and generate stronger brain activity than straight edges. The reason is probably that sharp curves and corners are less predictable and redundant (and therefore more novel and informative) than straight edges. By the same token, curved trajectories may be less redundant, and therefore more salient, than straight ones.

MULTISENSORY MISDIRECTION

Apollo Robbins (*below right*), who bills himself as a professional thief, demonstrates that misleading the "mark" to look in one direction keeps the mark from attending to his valuables. Robbins relies on the manipulation of touch and the mark's personal space as well as on misdirecting vision. An astonishing video of Robbins surreptitiously removing another man's wristwatch is available at **http://tinyurl.com/6lhxy8**

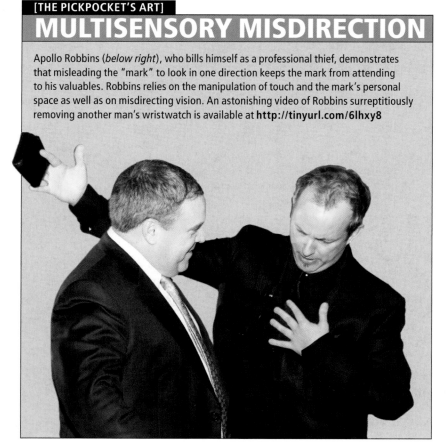

COURTESY OF APOLLO ROBBINS

[ILLUSORY CORRELATION]

HOW THE BRAIN DEALS WITH THE "IMPOSSIBLE"

Videos of magic tricks that seemed to portray impossible causal relations, such as making a ball vanish (*top row of photographs*), were shown to experimental subjects, while functional magnetic resonance images were made of the subjects' brains. A control group saw highly similar videos, except that no magic trick was performed (*bottom row*). The areas of the brain highlighted in color (*below right*) show where additional neural activity took place when the subjects viewed the magic videos instead of the control videos.

    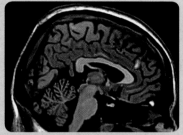

    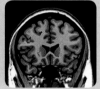

Controlling Awareness in the Wired Brain

The possibilities of using magic as a source of cognitive illusion to help isolate the neural circuits responsible for specific cognitive functions seem endless. Neuroscientists recently borrowed a technique from magic that made volunteer subjects incorrectly link two events as cause and effect while images of the subjects' brains were recorded. When event A precedes event B, we often conclude, rightly or wrongly, that A causes B. The skilled magician takes advantage of that predisposition by making sure that event A (say, pouring water on a ball) always precedes event B (the ball disappearing). In fact, A does not cause B, but its prior appearance helps the magician make it seem so. Cognitive psychologists call this kind of effect illusory correlation.

In an unpublished study in 2006 Kuhn and cognitive neuroscientists Ben A. Parris and Tim L. Hodgson, both then at the University of Exeter in England, showed videos of magic tricks that involved apparent violations of cause and effect to subjects undergoing functional magnetic resonance imaging. The subjects' brain images were compared with those of a control group: people who watched videos showing no apparent causal violations. The investigators found greater activation in the anterior cingulate cortex among the subjects who were watching magic tricks than among the controls. The finding suggests that this brain area may be important for interpreting causal relationships.

The work of Kuhn and his colleagues only begins to suggest the power of the techniques of magic for manipulating attention and awareness while studying the physiology of the brain. If neuroscientists learn to use the methods of magic with the same skill as professional magicians, they, too, should be able to control awareness precisely and in real time. If they correlate the content of that awareness with the functioning of neurons, they will have the means to explore some of the mysteries of consciousness itself. ∎

We Read Your Mind

We have removed your card!

Did we guess the card you picked on page 19? If so, does Pickover's ESP system explain our correct answer, or is there a simpler explanation? Read no further until you want to know the answer.

invisible when you take another look.
even a big, obvious change—can be all but
psychologists call change blindness. A change—
trick (most people do), you are a victim of what
circling an eye distracted you and you fell for the
pictured here. Notice any differences? If the act of
page 19, then compare them with the five cards
Give up? Look once more at the six cards on

➡ **MORE TO EXPLORE**

Failure to Detect Mismatches between Intention and Outcome in a Simple Decision Task. Petter Johansson, Lars Hall, Sverker Sikström and Andreas Olsson in *Science,* Vol. 310, pages 116–119; October 7, 2005.

Attention and Awareness in Stage Magic: Turning Tricks into Research. Stephen L. Macknik, Mac King, James Randi, Apollo Robbins, Teller, John Thompson and Susana Martinez-Conde in *Nature Reviews Neuroscience.* Advance online publication; July 30, 2008.

Microsaccades Drive Illusory Motion in the Enigma Illusion. Xoana G. Troncoso, Stephen L. Macknik, Jorge Otero-Millan, Susana Martinez-Conde in *Proceedings of the National Academy of Sciences USA,* Vol. 105, No. 41, pages 16033–16038; October 14, 2008.

For videos of leading magicians performing at the 2007 Magic of Consciousness Symposium, visit **www.mindscience.org/ magicsymposium**

Quiet! Sleeping Brain at Work

During slumber, our brain engages in data analysis, from strengthening memories to solving problems

By Robert Stickgold and Jeffrey M. Ellenbogen

In 1865 Friedrich August Kekulé woke up from a strange dream: he imagined a snake forming a circle and biting its own tail. Like many organic chemists of the time, Kekulé had been working feverishly to describe the true chemical structure of benzene, a problem that continually eluded understanding. But Kekulé's dream of a snake swallowing its tail, so the story goes, helped him to accurately realize that benzene's structure formed a ring. This insight paved the way for a new understanding of organic chemistry and earned Kekulé a title of nobility in Germany.

Although most of us have not been ennobled, there is something undeniably familiar about Kekulé's problem-solving method. Whether deciding to go to a particular college, accept a challenging job offer or propose to a future spouse, "sleeping on it" seems to provide the clarity we need to piece together life's puzzles. But how does slumber present us with answers?

The latest research suggests that while we are peacefully asleep our brain is busily processing the day's information. It combs through recently formed memories, stabilizing, copying and filing them, so that they will be more useful the next day. A night of sleep can make memories resistant to interference from other information and allow us to recall them for use more effectively the next morning. And sleep not only strengthens memories, it also lets the brain sift through newly formed memories, possibly even identifying what is worth keeping and selectively maintaining or enhancing these aspects of a memory. When a picture contains both emotional and unemotional elements, sleep can save the important emotional parts and let the less relevant background drift away. It can analyze collections of memories to discover relations among them or identify the gist of a memory while the unnecessary details fade—perhaps even helping us find the *meaning* in what we have learned.

Not Merely Resting

If you find this news surprising, you are not alone. Until the mid-1950s, scientists generally assumed that the brain was shut down while we snoozed. Although German psychologist Hermann Ebbinghaus had evidence in 1885 that

RICK GAYLE *Corbis* (*head and gears*); GETTY IMAGES (*background*)

The mystery of what happens during sleep has provoked many theories over the centuries.

sleep protects simple memories from decay, for decades researchers attributed the effect to a passive protection against interference. We forget things, they argued, because all the new information coming in pushes out the existing memories. But because there is nothing coming in while we get shut-eye, we simply do not forget as much.

Then, in 1953, the late physiologists Eugene Aserinsky and Nathaniel Kleitman of the University of Chicago discovered the rich variations in brain activity during sleep, and scientists realized they had been missing something important. Aserinsky and Kleitman found that our sleep fol-

lows a 90-minute cycle, in and out of rapid-eye-movement (REM) sleep. During REM sleep, our brain waves—the oscillating electromagnetic signals that result from large-scale brain activity—look similar to those produced while we are awake [*see illustration on opposite page*]. And in subsequent decades, the late Mircea Steriade of Laval University in Quebec and other neuroscientists discovered that individual collections of neurons were independently firing in between these REM phases, during periods known as slow-wave sleep, when large populations of brain cells fire synchronously in a steady rhythm of one to four beats each second. So it became clear that the sleeping brain was not merely "resting," either in REM sleep or in slow-wave sleep. Sleep was doing something different. Something *active*.

Sleep to Remember

The turning point in our understanding of sleep and memory came in 1994 in a ground-breaking study. Neurobiologists Avi Karni, Dov Sagi and their colleagues at the Weizmann Institute of Science in Israel showed that when volunteers got a night of sleep, they improved at a task that involved rapidly discriminating between objects they saw—but only when they had had normal amounts of REM sleep. When the subjects were deprived of REM sleep, the improvement disappeared. The fact that performance actually rose overnight negated the idea of passive protection. Something had to be happening within the sleeping brain that altered the memories formed the day before. But Karni and Sagi described REM sleep as a permissive state—one that *could* allow changes to happen—rather than a necessary one. They proposed that such unconscious improvements could happen across the day or the night. What was important, they argued, was that improvements could only occur during *part* of the night, during REM.

It was not until one of us (Stickgold) revisited this question in 2000 that it became clear that sleep could, in fact, be necessary for this improvement to occur. Using the same rapid visual discrimination task, we found that only with more than six hours of sleep did people's performance improve over the 24 hours following the learning session. And REM sleep was not the only important component: slow-wave sleep was equally crucial. In other words, sleep—in all its phases—does something to improve memory that being awake does not do.

To understand how that could be so, it helps to review a few memory basics. When we "en-

THE SLEEP OF REASON PRODUCES MONSTERS, BY FRANCISCO GOYA, © BRITISH MUSEUM/ART RESOURCE, NY

FAST FACTS
While We Are Sleeping

1 >> As we snooze, our brain is busily processing the information we have learned during the day.

2 >> Sleep makes memories stronger, and it even appears to weed out irrelevant details and background information so that only the important pieces remain.

3 >> Our brain also works during slumber to find hidden relations among memories and to solve problems we were working on while awake.

code" information in our brain, the newly minted memory is actually just beginning a long journey during which it will be stabilized, enhanced and qualitatively altered, until it bears only faint resemblance to its original form. Over the first few hours, a memory can become more stable, resistant to interference from competing memories. But over longer periods, the brain seems to decide what is important to remember and what is not—and a detailed memory evolves into something more like a story.

In 2006 we demonstrated the powerful ability of sleep to stabilize memories and provided further evidence against the myth that sleep only passively (and, therefore, transiently) protects memories from interference. We reasoned that if sleep merely provides a transient benefit for memory, then memories after sleep should be, once again, susceptible to interference. We first trained people to memorize pairs of words in an A-B pattern (for example, "blanket-window") and then allowed some of the volunteers to sleep.

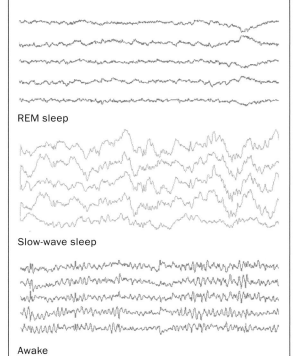

REM sleep

Slow-wave sleep

Awake

The discovery in 1953 of rapid-eye-movement sleep and its characteristic brain activity (*top*), detected with electro-encephalography, dispelled the notion that the brain simply rests during sleep. Soon after, slow-wave sleep patterns (*middle*) were discovered.

(Sleep, it seems, does something to **improve memory** that being awake does not do.)

Later they all learned pairs in an A-C pattern ("blanket-sneaker"), which were meant to interfere with their memories of the A-B pairs. As expected, the people who slept could remember more of the A-B pairs than people who had stayed awake could. And when we introduced interfering A-C pairs, it was even more apparent that those who slept had a stronger, more stable memory for the A-B sets. Sleep changed the memory, making it robust and more resistant to interference in the coming day.

But sleep's effects on memory are not limited to stabilization. Over just the past few years, a number of studies have demonstrated the sophistication of the memory processing that happens during slumber. In fact, it appears that as we sleep, the brain might even be dissecting our memories and retaining only the most salient details. In one study we created a series of pictures that included either unpleasant or neutral objects on a neutral background and then had people view the pictures one after another. Twelve hours later we tested their memories for the objects and the backgrounds. The results were quite surprising. Whether the subjects had stayed awake or slept, the accuracy of their memories

dropped by 10 percent for everything. Everything, that is, except for the memory of the emotionally evocative objects after a night of sleep. Instead of deteriorating, memories for the emotional objects actually seemed to improve by a few percent overnight, showing about a 15 percent improvement relative to the deteriorating backgrounds. After a few more nights, one could imagine that little but the emotional objects would be left. We know this culling happens over time with real-life events, but now it appears that sleep may play a crucial role in this evolution of emotional memories.

Precisely how the brain strengthens and enhances memories remains largely a mystery, although we can make some educated guesses at the basic mechanism. We know that memories are created by altering the strengths of connections among hundreds, thousands or perhaps even millions of neurons, making certain *patterns* of activity more likely to recur. These patterns of activity, when reactivated, lead to the recall of a memory—whether that memory is where we left the car keys or a pair of words such as "blanket-window." These changes in synaptic strength are thought to arise from a molecular process known as long-term potentiation, which strengthens the connections between pairs of neurons that fire at the same time. Thus, cells that fire together wire together, locking the pattern in place for future recall.

During sleep, the brain reactivates patterns of neural activity that it performed during the day, thus strengthening the memories by long-term potentiation. In 1994 neuroscientists Matthew Wilson and Bruce McNaughton, both then at the University of Arizona, showed this effect for the first time using rats fitted with implants that

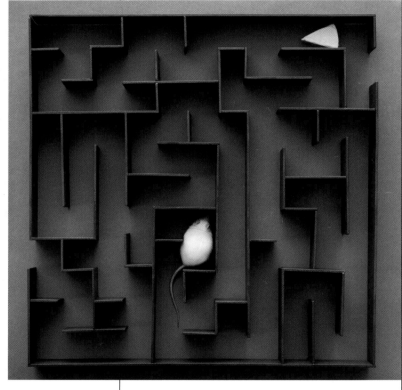

When a rat runs a maze, neurons in its brain called place cells are active as it traverses specific regions of the track. Later, as the rat sleeps, the same neurons fire—the rat rehearses its run of the maze while unconscious.

monitored their brain activity. They taught these rats to circle a track to find food, recording neuronal firing patterns from the rodents' brains all the while. Cells in the hippocampus—a brain structure critical for spatial memory—created a map of the track, with different "place cells" firing as the rats traversed each region of the track [see "The Matrix in Your Head," by James J. Knierim; SCIENTIFIC AMERICAN MIND, June/July 2007]. Place cells correspond so closely to exact physical locations that the researchers could monitor the rats' progress around the track

simply by watching which place cells were firing at any given time. And here is where it gets even more interesting: when Wilson and McNaughton continued to record from these place cells as the rats slept, they saw the cells continuing to fire in the same order—as if the rats were "practicing" running around the track in their sleep.

As this unconscious rehearsing strengthens memory, something more complex is happening as well—the brain may be selectively rehearsing the more difficult aspects of a task. For instance, Matthew P. Walker's work at Harvard Medical School in 2005 demonstrated that when subjects learned to type complicated sequences such as 4-1-3-2-4 on a keyboard (much like learning a new piano score), sleeping between practice sessions led to faster and more coordinated finger movements. But on more careful examination, he found that people were not simply getting faster overall on this typing task. Instead each subject was getting faster on those particular keystroke sequences at which he or she was worst.

The brain accomplishes this improvement, at least in part, by moving the memory for these sequences overnight. Using functional magnetic resonance imaging, Walker showed that his subjects used different brain regions to control their typing after they had slept [*see box on opposite page*]. The next day typing elicited more activity in the right primary motor cortex, medial prefrontal lobe, hippocampus and left cerebellum—places that would support faster and more precise key-press movements—and less activity in the parietal cortices, left insula, temporal pole and frontopolar region, areas whose suppression indicates reduced conscious and emotional effort. The entire memory got strengthened, but especially the parts that needed it most, and sleep was doing this work by using different parts of the brain than were used while learning the task.

Solutions in the Dark

These effects of sleep on memory are impressive. Adding to the excitement, recent discoveries show that sleep also facilitates the active analysis of new memories, enabling the brain to solve problems and infer new information. In 2007 one of us (Ellenbogen) showed that the brain learns while we are asleep. The study used a transitive inference task; for example, if Bill is older

Nocturnal Practice

When pianists learn a new score, they practice difficult runs again and again until the motions become second nature. Part of this internalizing process depends on sleep: a 2005 functional MRI study showed that when people snooze after they learn to type complicated sequences, different brain regions become involved in controlling the keystrokes.

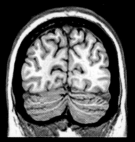
Left cerebellum

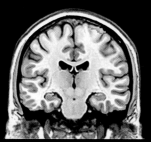
Right primary motor cortex

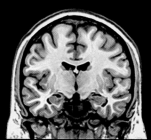
Right hippocampus

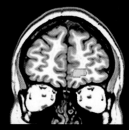
Right medial prefrontal cortex

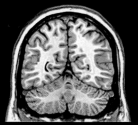
Parietal lobes

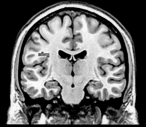
Left insula

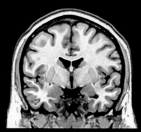
Left temporal pole

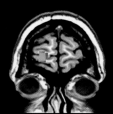
Left fronto-polar area

The brain regions indicated in yellow were more active during practice sessions after a night of sleep. These areas support faster typing and more precise keyboard movements—and indeed, subjects who slept improved their speed and accuracy more than did subjects who remained awake between rehearsals. The areas highlighted in blue were less active after sleep, indicating a reduction in conscious and emotional effort during the typing task.

than Carol and Carol is older than Pierre, the laws of transitivity make it clear that Bill is older than Pierre. Making this inference requires stitching those two fragments of information together. People and animals tend to make these transitive inferences without much conscious thought, and the ability to do so serves as an enormously helpful cognitive skill: we discover new information (Bill is older than Pierre) without ever learning it directly.

The inference seems obvious in Bill and Pierre's case, but in the experiment, we used abstract colored shapes that have no intuitive relation to one another [*see top illustration on next page*], making the task more challenging. We taught people so-called premise pairs—they learned to choose, for example, the orange oval over the turquoise one, turquoise over green, green over paisley, and so on. The premise pairs imply a hierarchy—if orange is a better choice than turquoise and turquoise is preferred to green, then orange should win over green. But when we

tested the subjects on these novel pairings 20 minutes after they learned the premise pairs, they had not yet discovered these hidden relations. They chose green just as often as they chose orange, performing no better than chance.

When we tested subjects 12 hours later on the same day, however, they made the correct choice 70 percent of the time. Simply allowing time to pass enabled the brain to calculate and learn these transitive inferences. And people who slept during the 12 hours performed significantly better, linking the most distant pairs (such as orange versus paisley) with 90 percent accuracy. So it seems the brain needs time after we learn information to process it, connecting

(The Authors)

ROBERT STICKGOLD is an associate professor at Harvard Medical School and Beth Israel Deaconess Medical Center in Boston. Also at Harvard, JEFFREY M. ELLENBOGEN is chief of the sleep division at Massachusetts General Hospital. Both study the interactions of sleep and cognition.

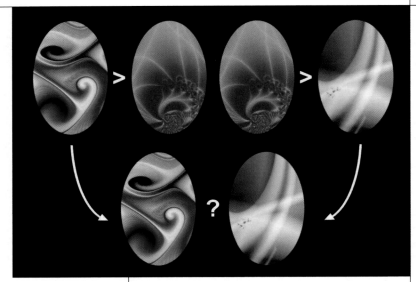

Through trial and error, study volunteers learned that orange is a better choice than turquoise, and turquoise is preferred to green. But only after time did they infer the hidden relation between orange and green, and with harder problems, sleep gave a distinct advantage.

the dots, so to speak—and sleep provides the maximum benefit.

In a 2004 study Ullrich Wagner and others in Jan Born's laboratory at the University of Lübeck in Germany elegantly demonstrated just how powerful sleep's processing of memories can be. They taught subjects how to solve a particular type of mathematical problem by using a long and tedious procedure and had them practice it about 100 times. The subjects were then sent away and told to come back 12 hours later, when they were instructed to try it another 200 times.

What the researchers had not told their subjects was that there is a much simpler way to solve these problems [see box below]. The researchers could tell if and when subjects gained insight into this shortcut, because their speed would suddenly increase. Many of the subjects did, in fact, discover the trick during the second session. But

when they got a night's worth of sleep between the two sessions, they were more than two and a half times more likely to figure it out—59 percent of the subjects who slept found the trick, compared with only 23 percent of those who stayed awake between the sessions. Somehow the sleeping brain was solving this problem, without even knowing that there was a problem to solve.

The Need to Sleep

As exciting findings such as these come in more and more rapidly, we are becoming sure of one thing: while we sleep, our brain is anything but inactive. It is now clear that sleep can consolidate memories by enhancing and stabilizing them and by finding patterns within studied material even when we do not know that patterns might be there. It is also obvious that skimping on sleep stymies these crucial cognitive processes: some aspects of memory consolidation only happen with more than six hours of sleep. Miss a night, and the day's memories might be compromised—an unsettling thought in our fast-paced, sleep-deprived society.

But the question remains: Why did we evolve in such a way that certain cognitive functions happen only while we are asleep? Would it not seem to make more sense to have these operations going on in the daytime? Part of the answer might be that the evolutionary pressures for sleep existed long before higher cognition—functions such as immune system regulation and efficient energy usage (for instance, hunt in the day and rest at night) are only two of the many reasons it makes sense to sleep on a planet that alternates between light and darkness. And because we al-

Sudden Insight

Researchers taught subjects to use two rules to solve a type of problem that consists of a series of ones, fours and nines: Starting from the left, look at the first two numbers. If they are the same, write this number down (*shown here in blue*). If they are different, write down the third possible number (for example, if they are a 1 and a 4, write down 9). Then take this intermediate (*blue*) number and the

next (*black*) number, and do it again. When you enter the final answer (*the red 9 here*), press the "Enter" key to tell the computer you're done.

What the subjects were not told is that the second-to-last unique number in the original series (*the black 9 just before the final 4 in this case*) will always be equivalent to the answer of the problem. After sleeping, most of the volunteers figured out the trick.　—*R.S. and J.M.E.*

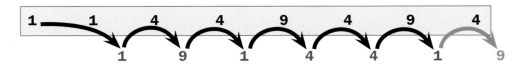

> The brain evolved to use **light and darkness** wisely: acquire information by day; process it by night.

We may be able to get by on as little as six hours of sleep a night, but closer to eight hours is better— and may optimize learning and memory performance.

JUPITERIMAGES

ready had evolutionary pressure to sleep, the theory goes, the brain evolved to use that time wisely by processing information from the previous day: acquire by day; process by night.

Or it might have been the other way around. Memory processing seems to be the only function of sleep that actually requires an organism to truly sleep—that is, to become unaware of its surroundings and stop processing incoming sensory signals. This unconscious cognition appears to demand the same brain resources used for processing incoming signals when awake. The brain, therefore, might have to shut off external inputs to get this job done. In contrast, although other functions such as immune system regulation might be more readily performed when an organism is inactive, there does not seem to be any reason why the organism would need to lose awareness. Thus, it may be these other functions that have been added to take advantage of the sleep that had already evolved for memory.

Many other questions remain about our nighttime cognition, however it might have evolved. Exactly how does the brain accomplish this memory processing? What are the chemical or molecular activities that account for these ef-

fects? These questions raise a larger issue about memory in general: What makes the brain remember certain pieces of information and forget others? We think the lesson here is that understanding sleep will ultimately help us to better understand memory.

The task might seem daunting, but these puzzles are the kind on which scientists thrive—and they can be answered. First, we will have to design and carry out more and more experiments, slowly teasing out answers. But equally important, we are going to have to sleep on it. **M**

(Further Reading)

◆ **Visual Discrimination Learning Requires Sleep after Training.** Robert Stickgold, LaTanya James and J. Allan Hobson in *Nature Neuroscience,* Vol. 3, No. 12, pages 1237–1238; December 2000.
◆ **Sleep Inspires Insight.** Ullrich Wagner, Steffen Gais, Hilde Haider, Rolf Verleger and Jan Born in *Nature,* Vol. 427, pages 352–355; January 22, 2004.
◆ **Sleep-Dependent Memory Consolidation.** Robert Stickgold in *Nature,* Vol. 437, pages 1272–1278; October 27, 2005.
◆ **Coordinated Memory Replay in the Visual Cortex and Hippocampus during Sleep.** Daoyun Ji and Matthew Wilson in *Nature Neuroscience,* Vol. 10, No. 1; January 2007.
◆ **Human Relational Memory Requires Time and Sleep.** J. M. Ellenbogen, P. Hu, J. D. Payne, D. Titone and M. P. Walker in *Proceedings of the National Academy of Sciences USA,* Vol. 104, No. 18, pages 7723–7728; May 2007.

The Secret to Raising Smart Kids

Hint: Don't tell your kids that they are. More than three decades of research shows that a focus on effort—not on intelligence or ability—is key to success in school and in life

By Carol S. Dweck

A brilliant student, Jonathan sailed through grade school. He completed his assignments easily and routinely earned As. Jonathan puzzled over why some of his classmates struggled, and his parents told him he had a special gift. In the seventh grade, however, Jonathan suddenly lost interest in school, refusing to do homework or study for tests. As a consequence, his grades plummeted. His parents tried to boost their son's confidence by assuring him that he was very smart. But their attempts failed to motivate Jonathan (who is a composite drawn from several children). Schoolwork, their son maintained, was boring and pointless.

Our society worships talent, and many people assume that possessing superior intel-

Young people who believe that their intelligence alone will enable them to succeed in school are often discouraged when the going gets tough.

ligence or ability—along with confidence in that ability—is a recipe for success. In fact, however, more than 30 years of scientific investigation suggests that an overemphasis on intellect or talent leaves people vulnerable to failure, fearful of challenges and unwilling to remedy their shortcomings.

The result plays out in children like Jonathan, who coast through the early grades under the dangerous notion that no-effort academic achievement defines them as smart or gifted. Such children hold an implicit belief that intelligence is innate and fixed, making striving to learn seem far less important than being (or looking) smart. This belief also makes them see challenges, mistakes and even the need to exert effort as threats to their ego rather than as opportunities to improve. And it causes them to lose confidence and motivation when the work is no longer easy for them.

Praising children's innate abilities, as Jonathan's parents did, reinforces this mind-set, which can also prevent young athletes or people in the workforce and even marriages from living up to their potential. On the other hand, our studies show that teaching people to have a "growth mind-set," which encourages a focus on effort rather than on intelligence or talent, helps make them into high achievers in school and in life.

The Opportunity of Defeat

I first began to investigate the underpinnings of human motivation—and how people persevere after setbacks—as a psychology graduate student at Yale University in the 1960s. Animal experiments by psychologists Martin Seligman, Steven Maier and Richard Solomon of the University of Pennsylvania had shown that after repeated failures, most animals conclude that a situation is hopeless and beyond their control. After such an experience, the researchers found, an animal often remains passive even when it can affect change—a state they called learned helplessness.

People can learn to be helpless, too, but not everyone reacts to setbacks this way. I wondered:

FAST FACTS
Growing Pains

1 >> Many people assume that superior intelligence or ability is a key to success. But more than three decades of research shows that an overemphasis on intellect or talent— and the implication that such traits are innate and fixed—leaves people vulnerable to failure, fearful of challenges and unmotivated to learn.

2 >> Teaching people to have a "growth mind-set," which encourages a focus on effort rather than on intelligence or talent, produces high achievers in school and in life.

3 >> Parents and teachers can engender a growth mind-set in children by praising them for their effort or persistence (rather than for their intelligence), by telling success stories that emphasize hard work and love of learning, and by teaching them about the brain as a learning machine.

JIM CUMMINS Getty Images (preceding pages); GETTY IMAGES (above)

FROM "IMPLICIT THEORIES OF INTELLIGENCE PREDICT ACHIEVEMENT ACROSS AN ADOLESCENT TRANSITION: A LONGITUDINAL STUDY AND AN INTERVENTION," BY L. S. BLACKWELL, K. H. TRZESNIEWSKI AND C. S. DWECK, IN *CHILD DEVELOPMENT*, VOL. 78, NO. 1; JANUARY/FEBRUARY 2007

Why do some students give up when they encounter difficulty, whereas others who are no more skilled continue to strive and learn? One answer, I soon discovered, lay in people's beliefs about *why* they had failed.

In particular, attributing poor performance to a lack of ability depresses motivation more than does the belief that lack of effort is to blame. In 1972, when I taught a group of elementary and middle school children who displayed helpless behavior in school that a lack of effort (rather than lack of ability) led to their mistakes on math problems, the kids learned to keep trying when the problems got tough. They also solved many of the problems even in the face of difficulty. Another group of helpless children who were simply rewarded for their success on easy problems did not improve their ability to solve hard math problems. These experiments were an early indication that a focus on effort can help resolve helplessness and engender success.

Subsequent studies revealed that the most persistent students do not ruminate about their own failure much at all but instead think of mistakes as problems to be solved. At the University of Illinois in the 1970s I, along with my then graduate student Carol Diener, asked 60 fifth graders to think out loud while they solved very difficult pattern-recognition problems. Some students reacted defensively to mistakes, denigrating their skills with comments such as "I never did have a good rememory," and their problem-solving strategies deteriorated.

Others, meanwhile, focused on fixing errors and honing their skills. One advised himself: "I should slow down and try to figure this out." Two schoolchildren were particularly inspiring. One, in the wake of difficulty, pulled up his chair, rubbed his hands together, smacked his lips and said, "I love a challenge!" The other, also confronting the hard problems, looked up at the experimenter and approvingly declared, "I was *hoping* this would be informative!" Predictably, the students with this attitude outperformed their cohorts in these studies.

Two Views of Intelligence

Several years later I developed a broader theory of what separates the two general classes of learners—helpless versus mastery-oriented. I re-alized that these different types of students not only explain their failures differently, but they also hold different "theories" of intelligence. The helpless ones believe that intelligence is a fixed trait: you have only a certain amount, and that's that. I call this a "fixed mind-set." Mistakes crack their self-confidence because they attribute errors to a lack of ability, which they feel powerless to change. They avoid challenges because challenges make mistakes more likely and looking smart less so. Like Jonathan, such children shun effort in the belief that having to work hard means they are dumb.

The mastery-oriented children, on the other hand, think intelligence is malleable and can be developed through education and hard work. They want to learn above all else. After all, if you believe that you can expand your intellectual skills, you want to do just that. Because slipups stem from a lack of effort, not ability, they can be remedied by more effort. Challenges are energizing rather than intimidating; they offer opportunities to learn. Students with such a growth

Mind-set and Math Grades

Students who believed that intelligence is malleable (*growth mind-set line*) earned higher math grades in the fall of seventh grade than those who believed in static intelligence (*fixed mind-set line*), even though the two groups had equivalent math achievement test scores in the sixth grade. The grades of the growth mind-set group then improved over the next two years, whereas the grades of the fixed mind-set students declined.

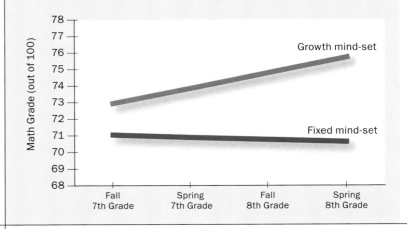

A for Effort

According to a survey we conducted in the mid-1990s, 85 percent of parents believed that praising children's ability or intelligence when they perform well is important for making them feel smart. But our work shows that praising a child's intelligence makes a child fragile and defensive. So, too, does generic praise that suggests a stable trait, such as "You are a good artist." Praise is very valuable, however, if it is carefully worded. Praise for the specific process a child used to accomplish something fosters motivation and confidence by focusing children on the actions that lead to success. Such process praise may involve commending effort, strategies, focus, persistence in the face of difficulty, and willingness to take on challenges. Here are some examples:

- You did a good job drawing. I like the detail you added to the people's faces.
- You really studied for your social studies test. You read the material over several times, outlined it and tested yourself on it. It really worked!
- I like the way you tried a lot of different strategies on that math problem until you finally got it.
- That was a hard English assignment, but you stuck with it until you got it done. You stayed at your desk and kept your concentration. That's great!
- I like that you took on that challenging project for your science class. It will take a lot of work—doing the research, designing the apparatus, making the parts and building it. You are going to learn a lot of great things.

Parents and teachers can also teach children to enjoy the process of learning by expressing positive views of challenges, effort and mistakes. Here are examples of such communications:

- Boy, this is hard—this is fun.
- Oh, sorry, that was too easy—no fun. Let's do something more challenging that you can learn from.
- Let's all talk about what we struggled with today and learned from. I'll go first.
- Mistakes are so interesting. Here's a wonderful mistake. Let's see what we can learn from it.   —C.S.D.

mind-set, we predicted, were destined for greater academic success and were quite likely to outperform their counterparts.

We validated these expectations in a study published in early 2007. Psychologists Lisa Blackwell of Columbia University and Kali H. Trzesniewski of Stanford University and I monitored 373 students for two years during the transition to junior high school, when the work gets more difficult and the grading more stringent, to determine how their mind-sets might affect their math grades. At the beginning of seventh grade, we assessed the students' mind-sets by asking them to agree or disagree with statements such as "Your intelligence is something very basic about you that you can't really change." We then assessed their beliefs about other aspects of learning and looked to see what happened to their grades.

As we had predicted, the students with a growth mind-set felt that learning was a more important goal in school than getting good grades. In addition, they held hard work in high regard, believing that the more you labored at something, the better you would become at it. They understood that even geniuses have to work hard for their great accomplishments. Confronted by a setback such as a disappointing test grade, students with a growth mind-set said they would study harder or try a different strategy for mastering the material.

The students who held a fixed mind-set, however, were concerned about looking smart with little regard for learning. They had negative views of effort, believing that having to work hard at something was a sign of low ability. They thought that a person with talent or intelligence did not need to work hard to do well. Attributing a bad grade to their own lack of ability, those with a fixed mind-set said that they would study *less* in the future, try never to take that subject again and consider cheating on future tests.

Such divergent outlooks had a dramatic impact on performance. At the start of junior high, the math achievement test scores of the students with a growth mind-set were comparable to those of students who displayed a fixed mind-set. But as the work became more difficult, the students with a growth mind-set showed greater persistence. As a result, their math grades overtook those of the other students by the end of the first semester—and the gap between the two groups continued to widen during the two years we followed them [*see box on page 35*].

Along with Columbia psychologist Heidi Grant, I found a similar relation between mind-set and achievement in a 2003 study of 128 Columbia freshman premed students who were enrolled in a challenging general chemistry course. Although all the students cared about grades, the ones who earned the best grades were those who placed a high premium on learning rather than on showing that they were smart in chemistry. The focus on learning strategies, effort and persistence paid off for these students.

Confronting Deficiencies

A belief in fixed intelligence also makes people less willing to admit to errors or to confront and remedy their deficiencies in school, at work and in their social relationships. In a study published in 1999 of 168 freshmen entering the University of Hong Kong, where all instruction and coursework are in English, three Hong Kong colleagues and I found that students with a growth mind-set who scored poorly on their English proficiency exam were far more inclined to take a remedial English course than were low-scoring students with a fixed mind-set. The students with a stagnant view of intelligence were presumably unwilling to admit to their deficit and thus passed up the opportunity to correct it.

A fixed mind-set can similarly hamper communication and progress in the workplace by leading managers and employees to discourage or ignore constructive criticism and advice. Research by psychologists Peter Heslin and Don VandeWalle of Southern Methodist University and Gary Latham of the University of Toronto shows that managers who have a fixed mind-set are less likely to seek or welcome feedback from their employees than are managers with a growth mind-set. Presumably, managers with a growth mind-set see themselves as works-in-progress and understand that they need feedback to improve, whereas bosses with a fixed mind-set are more likely to see criticism as reflecting their underlying

level of competence. Assuming that other people are not capable of changing either, executives with a fixed mind-set are also less likely to mentor their underlings. But after Heslin, VandeWalle and Latham gave managers a tutorial on the value and principles of the growth mind-set, supervisors became more willing to coach their employees and gave more useful advice.

Mind-set can affect the quality and longevity of personal relationships as well, through people's willingness—or unwillingness—to deal with difficulties. Those with a fixed mind-set are

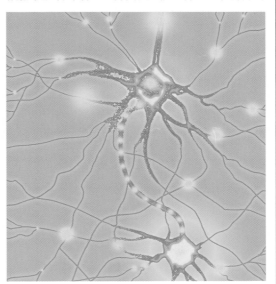

In tutorials that advance a growth mind-set, students discover that learning promotes the formation of new connections between neurons in the brain.

less likely than those with a growth mind-set to broach problems in their relationships and to try to solve them, according to a 2006 study I conducted with psychologist Lara Kammrath of Wilfrid Laurier University in Ontario. After all, if you think that human personality traits are more or less fixed, relationship repair seems largely futile. Individuals who believe people can change and grow, however, are more confident that confronting concerns in their relationships will lead to resolutions.

Proper Praise

How do we transmit a growth mind-set to our children? One way is by telling stories about achievements that result from hard work. For in-

(The Author)

CAROL S. DWECK is Lewis and Virginia Eaton Professor of Psychology at Stanford University. She has held professorships at Columbia University, the University of Illinois and Harvard University and is a member of the American Academy of Arts and Sciences. Her most recent book is *Mindset*, published by Random House in 2006.

MEHAU KULYK SPL/Photo Researchers, Inc.

stance, talking about math geniuses who were more or less born that way puts students in a fixed mind-set, but descriptions of great mathematicians who fell in love with math and developed amazing skills engenders a growth mind-set, our studies have shown. People also communicate mind-sets through praise [*see box on page 36*]. Although many, if not most, parents believe that they should build up a child by telling him or her how brilliant and talented he or she is, our research suggests that this is misguided.

In studies involving several hundred fifth graders published in 1998, for example, Columbia psychologist Claudia M. Mueller and I gave children questions from a nonverbal IQ test. After the first 10 problems, on which most children did fairly well, we praised them. We praised some of them for their intelligence: "Wow ... that's a really good score. You must be smart at this." We commended others for their effort: "Wow ... that's a really good score. You must have worked really hard."

We found that intelligence praise encouraged a fixed mind-set more often than did pats on the back for effort. Those congratulated for their intelligence, for example, shied away from a challenging assignment—they wanted an easy one instead—far more often than the kids applauded for their effort. (Most of those lauded for their hard work wanted the difficult problem set from which they would learn.) When we gave everyone hard problems anyway, those praised for being smart became discouraged, doubting their ability. And their scores, even on an easier problem

set we gave them afterward, declined as compared with their previous results on equivalent problems. In contrast, students praised for their effort did not lose confidence when faced with the harder questions, and their performance improved markedly on the easier problems that followed [*see box on opposite page*].

Making Up Your Mind-set

In addition to encouraging a growth mind-set through praise for effort, parents and teachers can help children by providing explicit instruction regarding the mind as a learning machine. Blackwell, Trzesniewski and I recently designed an eight-session workshop for 91 students whose math grades were declining in their first year of junior high. Forty-eight of the students received instruction in study skills only, whereas the others attended a combination of study skills sessions and classes in which they learned about the growth mind-set and how to apply it to schoolwork.

In the growth mind-set classes, students read and discussed an article entitled "You Can Grow Your Brain." They were taught that the brain is like a muscle that gets stronger with use and that learning prompts neurons in the brain to grow new connections. From such instruction, many students began to see themselves as agents of their own brain development. Students who had been disruptive or bored sat still and took note. One particularly unruly boy looked up during the discussion and said, "You mean I don't have to be dumb?"

As the semester progressed, the math grades of the kids who learned only study skills continued to

Chemist Marie Curie (*left*) and inventor Thomas A. Edison (*right*) developed their genius through passion and tremendous effort.

BETTMANN/CORBIS (*Curie and Edison*)

decline, whereas those of the students given the growth-mind-set training stopped falling and began to bounce back to their former levels. Despite being unaware that there were two types of instruction, teachers reported noticing significant motivational changes in 27 percent of the children in the growth mind-set workshop as compared with only 9 percent of students in the control group. One teacher wrote: "Your workshop has already had an effect. L [our unruly male student], who never puts in any extra effort and often doesn't turn in homework on time, actually stayed up late to finish an assignment early so I could review it and give him a chance to revise it. He earned a B+. (He had been getting Cs and lower.)"

Other researchers have replicated our results. Psychologists Catherine Good, then at Columbia, and Joshua Aronson and Michael Inzlicht of New York University reported in 2003 that a growth mind-set workshop raised the math and English achievement test scores of seventh graders. In a 2002 study Aronson, Good (then a graduate student at the University of Texas at Austin) and their colleagues found that college students began to enjoy their schoolwork more, value it more highly and get better grades as a result of training that fostered a growth mind-set.

We have now encapsulated such instruction in an interactive computer program called "Brainology," which should be more widely available by mid-2008. Its six modules teach students about the brain—what it does and how to make it work better. In a virtual brain lab, users can click on brain regions to determine their functions or on nerve endings to see how connections form when people learn. Users can also advise virtual students with problems as a way of practicing how to handle schoolwork difficulties; additionally, users keep an online journal of their study practices.

New York City seventh graders who tested a pilot version of Brainology told us that the program had changed their view of learning and how to promote it. One wrote: "My favorite thing from Brainology is the neurons part where when u [sic] learn something there are connections and they keep growing. I always picture them when I'm in school." A teacher said of the students who used the program: "They offer to practice, study, take notes, or pay attention to ensure that connections will be made."

Teaching children such information is not just a ploy to get them to study. People do differ in intelligence, talent and ability. And yet research is converging on the conclusion that great accom-

The Effects of Praise

Children praised for their intelligence solved significantly fewer problems after a failure than they had before encountering difficulty. In contrast, children praised for their effort solved *more* problems after their brush with adversity than they had before it.

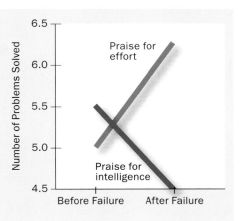

plishment, and even what we call genius, is typically the result of years of passion and dedication and not something that flows naturally from a gift. Mozart, Edison, Curie, Darwin and Cézanne were not simply born with talent; they cultivated it through tremendous and sustained effort. Similarly, hard work and discipline contribute much more to school achievement than IQ does.

Such lessons apply to almost every human endeavor. For instance, many young athletes value talent more than hard work and have consequently become unteachable. Similarly, many people accomplish little in their jobs without constant praise and encouragement to maintain their motivation. If we foster a growth mind-set in our homes and schools, however, we will give our children the tools to succeed in their pursuits and to become responsible employees and citizens. **M**

(Further Reading)

◆ **Praise for Intelligence Can Undermine Children's Motivation and Performance.** Claudia M. Mueller and Carol S. Dweck in *Journal of Personality and Social Psychology,* Vol. 75, No. 1, pages 33–52; November 1998.

◆ **Self-Discipline Outdoes IQ in Predicting Academic Performance of Adolescents.** A. Duckworth and M. Seligman in *Psychological Science,* Vol. 16, pages 939–944; 2005.

◆ **Why Do Beliefs about Intelligence Influence Learning Success? A Social Cognitive Neuroscience Model.** J. A. Mangels, B. Butterfield, J. Lamb, C. Good and C. S. Dweck in *Social Cognitive and Affective Neuroscience,* Vol. 1, No. 2, pages 75–86; September 2006.

◆ **The Cambridge Handbook of Expertise and Expert Performance.** Edited by K. A. Ericsson, N. Charness, P. J. Feltovich and R. R. Hoffman. Cambridge University Press, 2006.

◆ **Implicit Theories of Intelligence Predict Achievement across an Adolescent Transition: A Longitudinal Study and an Intervention.** Lisa S. Blackwell, Kali H. Trzesniewski and Carol S. Dweck in *Child Development,* Vol. 78, No. 1, pages 246–263; January/February 2007.

◆ **Subtle Linguistic Cues Affect Children's Motivation.** A. Cimpian, H.-M. C. Arce, E. M. Markman and C. S. Dweck in *Psychological Science,* Vol. 18, No. 4, pages 314–316; April 2007.

FROM "PRAISE FOR INTELLIGENCE CAN UNDERMINE CHILDREN'S MOTIVATION AND PERFORMANCE," BY C. M. MUELLER AND C. S. DWECK, IN *JOURNAL OF PERSONALITY AND SOCIAL PSYCHOLOGY*, VOL. 75, NO. 1; JULY 1998

Researchers are discovering the myriad ways in which language can have a profound effect on the choices we make—from the foods we eat to the laws we support

WHEN WORDS DECIDE

By Barry Schwartz

magine that the U.S. is preparing for an outbreak of an unusual Asian disease that is expected to kill 600 people. Government officials have proposed two alternative programs to combat the disease. Under program A, 200 people will be saved. Under B, there is a one-third probability that 600 people will be saved and a two-thirds probability that nobody will. Confronted by this choice, 72 percent of people choose A, preferring to save 200 people for certain rather than risking saving no one.

Now imagine that officials present these two options instead: under program C, 400 people will die; under program D, there is a one-third probability that nobody will die and a two-thirds probability that all 600 people will perish. Faced with this pair of scenarios, 78 percent of people choose D, according to results of a classic study by Nobel laureate Daniel Kahneman, a psychologist at Princeton University, and his longtime collaborator, psychologist Amos Tversky.

when the options are described as in C and D?

Kahneman and Tversky's research provides a clue: people respond to choices involving losses, such as deaths, differently from those relating to gains, such as survivors. When choosing between positive outcomes, people tend to be risk averse and want the sure thing (saving 200 people) but are far more willing to take risks when weighing losses—a psychological tendency that can be exploited by the deliberate wording of options. Some 30 years ago Kahneman and Tversky's initial findings in this field launched a concerted inquiry into how the framing of options affects people's decisions. Since then, they and many others have discovered various ways in which language can have a profound—and often counterintuitive—effect on the choices people make.

In addition to the loss-versus-gain effect, recent research shows, for example, that people can be moved en masse to opt for one alternative when it is positioned as the default—an unstated option that people get if they do not make a selection. But pick a different default and a crowd moves the other way, as if magnetically motivated to follow the unmarked road. People's decisions can be subtly influenced by context as well. Pitting one selection against a costlier or more frivolous alternative can make that choice seem more attractive than if it had been matched against a more favorable option.

We all seem rather fickle. Indeed, studies on the psychology of choice somewhat radically imply that we do not strictly possess preferences and values; instead we construct them in response to the questions the world asks us or the choices it presents us. The apparent capriciousness of our opinions often appears irrational, but in some cases there is a funny logic to it: descriptions may influence not only what we choose but also how we enjoy or appreciate that choice—a circular way of making that option the "right" one for us [see box on page 46].

Understanding how words steer our decisions regarding gains and losses can help guide the phrasing of public service announcements to best motivate people to, say, conserve energy or take care of their health. In other situations, officials might employ the power of defaults to lead people toward options they are likely to prefer, even if they tend not to choose them out of laziness, hurriedness or misunderstanding. And finally, an awareness of contextual wording traps may enable all of us to reconsider our reactions toward surveys, political campaigns and clever advertisements, recognizing that almost every ques-

Of course, these two pairs of options—A or B and C or D—are identical: saving 200 lives means that 400 people will die, and in both B and D, taking a one-third chance to save everyone means taking a two-thirds chance to lose everyone. Whichever choice you make, logic would seem to dictate that it should be the same no matter how the options are worded. So why do people tend to prefer A to B but the reverse

JIM FRAZIER Getty Images

Risky Choices

People respond differently to options describing gains than to those that refer to losses. This tendency, which is explained by something called prospect theory, can result in logically inconsistent decisions. In this depiction of the theory (*graph*), which was co-developed nearly 30 years ago by Nobel laureate Daniel Kahneman, a psychologist at Princeton University, and his longtime collaborator, psychologist Amos Tversky, the *x*-axis plots the objective state of affairs, from negative, for instance, number of lives lost, through neutral (zero) to positive, say, number of lives saved. The *y*-axis plots people's subjective responses to the various objective states—that is, how good or bad these realities make people feel.

The curve in the upper right quadrant captures how people respond to positives, or gains, and its shape portrays the economic principle of diminishing marginal utility. Saving 600 lives will not feel three times as good as saving 200 lives, so people do not want to take a risk to save all 600 people. The lower left quadrant shows how people respond to negatives, or losses, and depicts the diminishing marginal disutility of losses. Because losing 600 lives will not hurt three times as much as losing 200, people feel good about taking the risk to lose nobody. People tend to seek risk more readily when making decisions about losses.

Whether decisions are described by the top right or the bottom left part of the curve depends on how the op-

tions are framed. Thus, people are unwilling to take a risk if the phrasing emphasizes positive outcomes, but they may flip to a riskier option if the words express the darker side of a picture. Notice, too, that the loss portion of the curve is about twice as steep as the gain portion, meaning that a loss of, say, $100 hurts worse than a gain of $100 feels good. All in all, people will be more motivated to avoid losses than to secure gains.

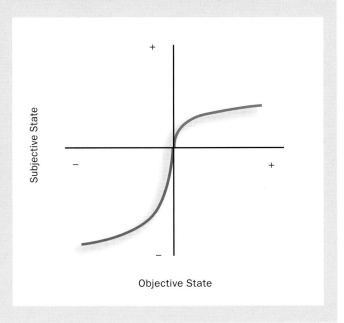

tion inexorably biases respondents toward one choice over another.

Gains and Losses

In their landmark research, Kahneman and Tversky pioneered the notion that two ways of describing a choice that are logically equivalent, as in the example above, are not necessarily psychologically equivalent. In something they called "prospect theory," Kahneman and Tversky deciphered the relation between the objective and the subjective as it relates to losses and gains.

Although people do become more satisfied as an outcome gets increasingly favorable, a person's happiness does not increase in linear fashion in relation to the gain, according to prospect theory [*see box above*]. Instead a person's subjective state improves at an increasingly slower rate until an objective improvement in a situation hardly changes a person's satisfaction at all—something economists call "diminishing marginal utility." This means, for example, that sav-

ing 600 lives will not feel three times as good as saving 200 lives—so taking a risk to save all 600 people feels like a bad psychological bet. Kahneman and Tversky argued that most people are risk averse when contemplating gains.

When it comes to negative occurrences, such as deaths, changes in a person's emotional state similarly diminish as the situation worsens rather than continuing to worsen at a rate proportional to the circumstances. Thus, losing 600 lives will not hurt three times as much as losing 200 would, so taking the risk to lose no one feels like a good psychological bet. This principle causes people to seek risk when it comes to losses.

And whether people are attending to gains or losses depends on how the options are framed. In the A-versus-B choice people are considering gains, whereas they are pondering losses when faced with the C-versus-D scenario, explaining why people are not willing to take a risk in the first situation but are in the second.

Prospect theory also holds that people actu-

more than 90 percent of the people in many European countries are organ donors, whereas only about 25 percent of Americans are—despite the fact that most Americans approve of organ donation. Why? In the U.S., to be an organ donor you have to sign a form. If you do not sign the form, you are not an organ donor. The latter is the default option, and that is the one most people choose. In much of Europe, the default option is the opposite of the U.S. default—you are an organ donor unless you indicate you do not want to be, so most Europeans make the reverse choice [*see box on opposite page*].

When employers switch procedures for voluntary 401(k) participation from opt-in (you have to sign a form to contribute to the plan) to opt-out (you have to sign a form to decline participation) initial enrollments jump from 49 to 86 percent, according to a 2001 study by University of Pennsylvania economist Brigitte Madrian and Dennis Shea of the United Health Group. And in a real-world experiment, the states of New Jersey and Pennsylvania simultaneously started to offer lower-cost, no-fault auto insurance. These policies restrict the right to sue while requiring insurance

(Wording public service pleas to focus on losses can motivate people to save energy or monitor their health.)

ally feel worse about a loss of a given amount than they would feel good about a gain of a similar magnitude. That means getting people to focus on avoiding losses when they make decisions will be more motivational than getting them to focus on securing gains. This fact can be exploited. Appeals to women to do breast self-exams that emphasize the benefits of early cancer detection (gains) are less effective than those that emphasize the costs of late detection (losses). Pleas to homeowners to conserve energy that focus on savings (gains) in utility bills are less powerful than efforts that focus on the added costs of using energy profligately (losses).

The Power of Silence

Another powerful way to influence choice is to leave something unsaid. In the U.S. and many European countries, people who renew their driver's license are asked if they want to be an organ donor. As decision scientists Eric J. Johnson of Columbia University and Daniel Goldstein, now at London Business School, reported in 2003,

companies to pay regardless of who is at fault in an accident. In New Jersey—but not in Pennsylvania—no-fault insurance was the default. As Columbia's Johnson and his colleagues reported in the *Journal of Risk and Uncertainty* in 1993, almost 80 percent of car owners in each state ended up with the default. The choice of default has cost Pennsylvanians millions of dollars over the years.

Why do defaults have such power? Some of it may come from inattention. Life is busy and complicated, and it is not possible to pay attention to everything. That is why most of us keep our cell phone plan whether or not it is the best one for us. Researching alternatives is time-consuming, and we do not want to be bothered. But laziness and inattention are not the sole reasons for the power of defaults. As University of California, San Diego, psychologist Craig R. M. McKenzie and his colleagues showed in a 2006 study, most people infer that the default is the recommended option.

Given the power of defaults, policymakers

JIM FRAZIER Getty Images

To Be—or Not to Be—an Organ Donor

SOURCE: "DO DEFAULTS SAVE LIVES?" BY E. J. JOHNSON AND D. GOLDSTEIN, IN SCIENCE, VOL. 302: NOVEMBER 21, 2003

Many more people effectively agree to be organ donors in countries that have opt-out policies (*green*), in which being an organ donor is the default, than in countries such as the U.S. that have opt-in policies (*gold*), in which people are not organ donors unless they take action.

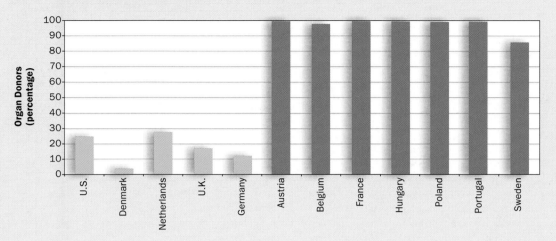

could use them to nudge people in a direction that will enhance their well-being, something University of Chicago legal scholar Cass R. Sunstein and economist Richard Thaler call "libertarian paternalism." In this practice, leaders would choose defaults with an eye on people's stated or implied preferences (the "paternalistic" part) while allowing anyone to opt out (the "libertarian" element).

Although you cannot always know what people's preferences are, you can often discern them. In the example of 401(k) plans, we can surmise a desire to participate because we know that people are more likely to sign up the longer they stay in their job, as if they have been meaning to do it but have been putting it off. Knowing whether Pennsylvanians or New Jersey residents are getting what they really want for car insurance is harder to determine. But given that it is nearly impossible to present options in a neutral fashion, why not prod people in a direction that makes most of them better off?

Matchmaker

Yet a third major influence of framing on choice is context. The attractiveness of an option will frequently depend on what it is compared with. Some years ago the gourmet food and kitchen gadget purveyor Williams-Sonoma introduced a new product: an automatic bread maker. You just throw the ingredients in, push a button, and several hours later you have a loaf of bread. The device sold for $275. Was $275 a lot to spend on a bread maker? That price was hard to judge because no similar products were then on the market. Months later Williams-Sonoma introduced a "deluxe" bread maker that sold for $429. Sales of the regular bread maker shot up—because the new, more expensive bread maker made the regular one look like a good deal.

Effects like this are pervasive. In research reported in 2002, University of Oregon psychologist Paul Slovic asked a group of people how much they would pay in taxes for an airport safety measure that would save 98 percent of 150 people at risk a year. Then he asked a second group how much they would pay to save 150 people a year. The first group would pay more for the measure than the second group would. Why? After all, saving 100 percent of 150 people is more beneficial than saving 98 percent of 150 people. But when the number 150 has no context, people will consider a broad variety of ways to spend money, many of them affecting thousands or millions of people. On the other hand, giving the 98 percent success rate restricts the context of the question and seems impressive, so people see intervention as quite cost-effective.

(The Author)

BARRY SCHWARTZ is a professor of psychology at Swarthmore College, where he has taught since 1971. He is author of *The Paradox of Choice: Why More Is Less* (Ecco, 2004).

Taste Tests

The language of choice not only affects what we choose but also—eerily—our sensory experiences of that choice. For example, people will choose a hamburger that is 75 percent lean over one that is 25 percent fat. But then, when they actually taste the two hamburgers (which are, of course, two versions of the same hamburger), the 75 percent lean burger actually tastes better. So although it may seem irrational to prefer one hamburger over another physically identical one, if the burger that is called "75 percent lean" tastes better than the one dubbed "25 percent fat," perhaps it makes sense to prefer that one, after all.

Other examples of food labels influencing our taste buds abound. Perrier is preferred to plain seltzer if both beverages are consumed with their labels showing, but otherwise tasters have no preference. Consumers judge protein nutrition bars that contain "soy protein" as grainier and less flavorful than when the word "soy" is removed from the description. They eat more vanilla ice cream if it is labeled "high fat" than if it is falsely labeled "low fat," which is, oddly, the opposite preference than the one they express for burgers, for which fat may signify "greasy."

And people prefer beer adulterated with balsamic vinegar labeled "MIT brew" to plain beer if they do not know about the adulteration or if they find out about the strange recipe after they have tasted the beers. The preference flips only if people know the beer has vinegar in it before they taste it, according to a 2006 study by Columbia University Business School professor Leonard Lee and Massachusetts Institute of Technology researchers Shane Frederick and Dan Ariely. Thus, what you know or think you know about a food will affect how it tastes, and getting

Consumers prefer Perrier to plain seltzer only if they see the Perrier label.

new information after the fact does not cause you to revise your memory of the taste. Labels and descriptions affect not only decisions but also how people experience the results of those decisions.

Are such preferences irrational? The point of choosing a burger, an ice cream or a beer, after all, is to enjoy it. And if you will enjoy "lean" burgers more than "fatty" ones, there is nothing wrong with having choices be affected by descriptions.

Your feelings about a decision are far less significant in other situations, of course. When a choice is about containing a disease, for example, how you feel should be irrelevant; what matters is what happens to the sick people. When choosing between public policies, your feelings about the policies are less important than the effects they will have. But the whole point of deciding what to eat—especially when the two items are nutritionally identical—is how you will feel about eating it. —*B.S.*

In another example of this phenomenon, Kahneman, Sunstein and their colleagues questioned a group of people about how much they would be willing to donate to a fund to reverse or prevent ecological disasters such as the loss of coral reefs and the endangerment of dolphins. Another group was asked how much they would be willing to pay to a program preventing skin cancer among farm workers. Surprisingly, the researchers found that people were willing to pay the same amount to save dolphins as to prevent skin cancer! But when they pitted dolphins and skin cancer directly against each other for a third group, the respondents were willing to spend vastly more money on skin cancer than on dolphins.

What is going on here? When people weigh saving dolphins against other ecological problems, dolphins rate high (they are so cute and so smart), so people will spend lots of money to save them. In contrast, skin cancer ranks low in priority on a list of serious health problems, so people choose to allocate relatively little money for it. But when dolphins and skin cancer appear on the same mental screen, people see skin cancer as

A "death tax" is far less popular than an "inheritance tax," even though these terms refer to the same tax.

much more worthy of resources. This change in public opinion occurs because when the options are framed narrowly, people decide within that limited context, comparing dolphin conservation only with other ecological issues and skin cancer only to other health issues. They lack a broad mental framework that could be used to contrast and evaluate divergent types of policies.

Thus, a more narrowly constructed question can raise a lower-priority project to greater prominence in people's minds, whereas if a public policy choice provides a more expansive framework, individuals can be subtly coaxed to reprioritize. Controlling the frame in a public policy debate can therefore sway the tide of public opinion in whatever direction the framers might prefer.

True Lies

All of this raises a key question: Do people actually know what they want? When faced with a decision, we imagine ourselves rationally considering our preferences and finding the option that best satisfies them. But research on how language affects decisions suggests otherwise. Instead of possessing preferences and values, we may simply create them when we are asked to make a decision. And, as we have seen, values and preferences can bend under the force of the question's wording. Thus, it is extremely difficult to discern people's "true" values and preferences, if they even exist.

Think about the public attitude toward the estate tax—a hefty tax on the assets of wealthy people when they die. This is a tax paid by a tiny handful of people—the most affluent group in the U.S. Yet a majority of Americans oppose it and support President George W. Bush's efforts to abolish it. What explains this peculiar public attitude? Is it that every American expects to be rich one day? I don't think so.

When Bush and his allies in Washington launched their campaign against the estate tax, they relabeled it the "death tax." Think of what this label does. Who pays the death tax? The dead person does. As if dying were not bad enough, the government reaches into the grave to extract its pound of silver. Worse yet, the dead person has already paid taxes on that money, when it was originally earned. Now suppose that instead of calling it a "death tax," we called it an "inheritance tax." Who pays the inheritance tax? The living do—and, unlike the dead, they have never paid taxes on these assets before. The same tax seems much more attractive and fair under that label.

So what do people *really* think about this tax? Such a seemingly straightforward question is actually exceedingly difficult to answer. When evaluating almost anything, we are at the mercy of its framing or context. We may search in vain for a neutral way to describe policies and products alike, and our failures will have significant effects on decisions of all types. If we are vigilant about monitoring how options are packaged, we might sometimes be able to diagnose framing effects and counteract them. But we will never catch them all. M

(Further Reading)

◆ **Choices, Values, and Frames.** Daniel Kahneman and Amos Tversky in *American Psychologist,* Vol. 39, No. 4, pages 341–350; April 1984.

◆ **The Construction of Preference.** P. Slovic in *American Psychologist,* Vol. 50, No. 5, pages 364–371; May 1995.

◆ **Mental Accounting Matters.** R. H. Thaler in *Journal of Behavioral Decision Making,* Vol. 12, No. 3, pages 183–206; September 1999.

◆ **Do Defaults Save Lives?** Eric J. Johnson and Daniel Goldstein in *Science,* Vol. 302, pages 1338–1339; November 21, 2003.

◆ **Libertarian Paternalism Is Not an Oxymoron.** C. R. Sunstein and R. H. Thaler in *University of Chicago Law Review,* Vol. 70, No. 4, pages 1159–1202; Fall 2003.

◆ **Try It, You'll Like It.** L. Lee, S. Frederick and D. Ariely in *Psychological Science,* Vol. 17, No. 12, pages 1054–1058; 2006.

◆ **"Leaky" Rationality: How Research on Behavioral Decision Making Challenges Normative Standards of Rationality.** D. J. Keys and B. Schwartz in *Perspectives on Psychological Science,* Vol. 2, No. 2, pages 162–180; June 2007.

A LOOK TELLS ALL

A person's face will always reveal his true feelings— if, like Paul Ekman, you are quick enough to recognize microexpressions

By Siri Schubert

Paul Ekman: Read my face.

W e do it automatically. As soon as we observe another person, we try to read his or her face for signs of happiness, sorrow, anxiety, anger. Sometimes we are right, sometimes we are wrong, and errors can create some sticky personal situations. Yet Paul Ekman is almost always right. The psychology professor emeritus at the University of California, San Francisco, has spent 40 years studying human facial expressions. He has catalogued more than 10,000 possible combinations of fa-

COURTESY OF PAUL EKMAN

GETTY IMAGES

cial muscle movements that reveal what a person is feeling inside. And he has taught himself how to catch the fleeting involuntary changes, called microexpressions, that flit across even the best liar's face, exposing the truth behind what he or she is trying to hide.

Ekman, 72, lives in Oakland, Calif., in a bright and airy house near the bay. As I talked with him there, he studied me, his eyes peering out from under bushy brows as if they were registering each brief facial tic I unknowingly exhibited. Does his tal-

ent make him a mind reader? "No," he says candidly. "The most I can do is tell how you are feeling at the moment but not what you are thinking." He is not being modest or coy; he is simply addressing the psychological bottom line behind facial expressions: "Anxiety always looks like anxiety," he explains, "regardless of whether a person fears that I'm seeing through their lie or that I don't believe them when they're telling the truth."

The professor calls the ever present risk we all take of misreading a person's visage

"Othello's error." In Shakespeare's drama, Othello misinterprets the fear in his wife Desdemona's face as a sign of her supposed infidelity. In truth, the poor woman is genuinely alarmed at her husband's unjust, jealous rage. Othello's subsequent decision to kill Desdemona is a fatal error, and Ekman wants to make sure that police, security personnel and secret service agents do not make the same mistake. "Arresting the guilty is a good thing," he acknowledges, "but decreasing the number of innocent people who are falsely accused is just as important." His system for understanding the emotions that faces portray,

understand why some people had little trouble decoding the feelings of others, almost as if they were reading an open book, whereas others fell for one con artist after another. His motto was: trust your eyes, not conventional wisdom. The widespread belief then was that facial expressions arose simply from cultural learning: a child in a given culture learned the faces that accompanied particular emotions by observing people, and over time different cultures developed different expressions. Even renowned researchers such as anthropologist Margaret Mead were unconvinced of the existence of a universal repertoire

Expressions can speak volumes, although they are open to interpretation. Is he hesitant, doubtful, concerned?

and his expertise in applying it, could help all kinds of law-enforcement and legal personnel in their work. It could also help the rest of us better negotiate how our family members, friends and colleagues really feel.

Face Code Deciphered

The very fact that psychologists are studying the emotion of facial expressions at all is due in large measure to Ekman's work. When he began studying psychology at the University of Chicago in the 1950s, emotions were a neglected subject at the periphery of the discipline. Many researchers believed that an individual's emotional world was inaccessible to scientific scrutiny—or at least was less interesting than, say, the mechanisms of learning and thinking or the motivations behind human actions.

Ekman, however, was fascinated by the mystery of nonverbal communication. He wanted to

of expressions, as Charles Darwin had proposed in his book *The Expression of the Emotions in Man and Animals,* published in 1872 but subsequently ignored.

To test his own hunch, Ekman headed for Brazil with a stack of photographs in his suitcase. The portraits showed sad, angry, happy or disgusted faces of white Americans, yet Brazilian college students had no trouble identifying the feelings depicted. Expeditions to Chile, Argentina and Japan generated the same results; regardless of where he went, local people seemed to understand, and use, the same facial expressions as the North Americans.

Concerned that perhaps inhabitants of "modern" societies had somehow cross-pollinated their facial movements, Ekman in 1967 visited extremely isolated tribes living in the jungles on the island of New Guinea. There again, though, he found that the basic emotions he had postulated,

GINA GORNY *Gehirn & Geist*

such as happiness, sadness, anger, fear, surprise and disgust, were associated with universal facial expressions. The excursion sealed it for him: the language of the face has biological origins, and culture has no significant effect on it.

This recognition raised a whole new set of questions. How many different facial expressions are human beings capable of? What precisely does a particular expression signify? Is it possible to learn how to read emotions? Ekman decided to create a sort of common dictionary of facial expressions, and he set about doing so with a mixture of meticulousness and daring.

"If I had known how long it would take to set up such a system, I might never have begun," he says now, with a slight sigh. "At the time, we didn't even know whether a person can make the same expression twice—whether his expressions always differ, even if only in minor ways."

Perceiving Microexpressions

Ekman and his U.C.S.F. colleague psychologist Wallace Friesen spent six years formulating their Facial Action Coding System (FACS), which they published in 1978. The system makes it possible to describe and classify any facial expression based on a combination of 43 facial-action units [see box on next page]. The 43 elements yield more than 10,000 possible combinations. Ekman and Friesen catalogued each combination by a FACS number, the Latin names for the muscles involved and the associated emotion, if any. For example: "1; inner brow raiser; frontalis, pars medialis," is one element of sadness.

One interesting aspect of this inventory is that many muscle combinations signify absolutely nothing. Ekman discovered another interesting phenomenon after spending the day in his laboratory trying to reproduce a convincing look of sadness: that evening he realized that he was feeling depressed. He then found that if he spent time engaged in imitating the components that make up a smile, his mood lifted. "That was like an epiphany," he recalls. It contradicted the naive notion that feelings originate solely in the psyche and that the body merely communicates them outwardly.

Ekman and Friesen were able to demonstrate that the coordinated tightening of certain facial muscles not only affected blood pressure and pulse rate but also could trigger the corresponding emotion. It seemed clear that a feedback mechanism was at work between the facial muscles and the brain's emotion centers.

Such a linkage caught the attention of psychologists, and by the early 1980s FACS started to be applied to real-world situations. Practitioners wanted to know how they might ascertain whether their patients were telling the truth by watching their faces. Such a talent could be critical, as an old videotape Ekman had made proved. The tape showed a psychiatric patient named Mary, who, apparently recovered from a severe bout of depression, begged her treating physician to allow her to spend the weekend at home. The doctor approved her request, but luckily before leaving, Mary admitted that she had planned to commit suicide.

Ekman had already studied the tape; he told viewers that if facial expressions indeed unveil a person's true feelings, they should be able to read Mary's intentions. Most viewers did not see the telltale sign at first, so Ekman pointed it out. He originally had watched the video over and over, often in slow motion so as not to miss even the slightest detail. And suddenly he saw it: for the briefest moment, a look of sheer desperation could be seen flitting across Mary's face. Such microexpressions—which often last no more than a fifth of a second—were the key. Regardless of how stoic we try to look or how heartily we laugh off a situation, the control that we can exert over our own facial features has its limits. Our true feelings always leak out, even if only for an instant.

When he discovered microexpressions, Ekman was teaching at U.C.S.F., and he spent several years putting together a self-teaching program that enabled people to decode faces according to the FACS system. By paying close attention to microexpressions, people can learn to read signals that previously would have been perceptible only in slow motion. And here Ekman hit

(The Author)

SIRI SCHUBERT is a freelance journalist living in San Francisco who writes for a variety of magazines.

on another interesting phenomenon: most people—including law students, police officers, judges and prosecuting attorneys—find it difficult to expose fakers, but a small number of people seem to be able to correctly interpret microexpressions intuitively. Apparently, some of us are born with handy lie detectors.

This capability should make more than a few fibbers—kids, criminals and politicians among them—very uneasy. On the other hand, certain individuals can learn to be convincing prevaricators. "Think of a chess player who controls his emotions and sets his facial expression so the other player will interpret it in a certain way," Ekman suggests. In addition, the more an individual believes his or her own fabrications, and the more often he or she serves them up successfully, the more difficult it will be for others to see through the deception. "Lies that are being told for the first time and that have an emotional component are the easiest to expose," Ekman says. That is why he recommends that interrogators ask their questions quickly and with an element of surprise. For example, instead of asking, "Were you in the parking lot of the Wal-Mart yesterday evening at six o'clock?" it is better to ask, "Where do you usually buy household items?"

Hard Truth

Although it is possible to learn to recognize microexpressions, Ekman warns against using them as a clear-cut indicator of a lie. Whenever he trains security personnel, he emphasizes the importance of asking a suspect how what the person just said made him or her feel. The response will make it less likely that an investigator will commit Othello's error. In addition, questioners need to pay attention to details other than facial expres-

Decoding Faces

In the 1970s Paul Ekman and Wallace Friesen developed the Facial Action Coding System, a tool kit for describing human facial expressions that can also reveal their emotional content. The system defines the contraction of individual facial muscles as so-called action units and assigns an emotional correlate to each one. For example, contraction of the orbicular eye muscles (c) accompanies every true smile. Contraction of the levator labii superioris alaeque nasi muscle (e) indicates disgust. Although there are 43 action units, robots and animated beings can reproduce many lifelike expressions using these two and eight others: the frontal muscles (a), corrugator muscles (b), eyelid muscles (d), zygomatic muscles and lifters (f), depressor anguli oris (g), orbicularis oris (h), depressor labii inferioris (i) and mentalis (j).   —S.S.

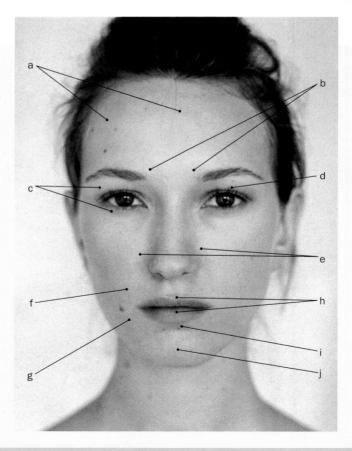

CORBIS

sion, such as small shifts in posture, speech or hand gestures, all of which could indicate a fabrication. Unless the suspect is Pinocchio, there is no unambiguous proof of a lie.

As to why so many people find it difficult to recognize deception, Ekman says, "Many people simply want to believe what they are being told, even if they really know better. Who wants to find out that your spouse is being unfaithful with your best friend? Or that your kids are using hard drugs? You should want to, but it's terrible when you discover it. And if you knew this, you'd have to do something about it; most of us are pretty avoidant."

From an evolutionary perspective, it would not necessarily have been advantageous for humans to be perfect lie detectors. In small, close-knit groups, little falsehoods are frequent and help group members gloss over unimportant mishaps or inequities. If every lie was singled out, the resulting confrontations would almost certainly do more harm than good. In the end, the smooth talkers would probably be expelled from the group, weakening its number if nothing else, and none of those remaining would have gained any benefit from the expulsion.

When it comes to hunting down terrorists, however, the ability to unmask has real survival implications. Ekman spends a great deal of time training antiterror specialists, even though he has been retired for over two years. Nevertheless, he is well aware of the narrow scope of his methods. "The tools I have to offer are pretty modest," he notes.

He also sees parallels between his work and that of the Dalai Lama, whom he has met several times at conferences. Like the spiritual leader, Ekman wants to help people understand their own feelings and master their impulses. "The only area where I differ with the Dalai Lama is on the issue of reincarnation," he muses.

Before we end our discussion at his home, I ask him about his own relationship to the truth. Ekman considers the question for a moment. "I have a golden rule," he responds, "according to which I decide when a lie is permitted. I ask myself how the other person would feel if he found out that he had been lied to." If the person would feel betrayed or taken advantage of, then the lie would be damaging.

Vigilantly offering the truth at every daily interaction and social occasion, though, may be of little value. "Would you tell your hosts that you were bored out of your mind at their party?" Ekman asks. "You see, no one would expect that—not even from an expert on lying." M

Sometimes emotions seem clear: happy, disgusted, surprised. Or is she smiling nervously, perhaps pained, feeling confronted?

(Further Reading)

◆ **The Naked Face.** Malcolm Gladwell in *The New Yorker,* pages 38–49; August 5, 2002.
◆ **Emotions Revealed: Recognizing Faces and Feelings to Improve Communication and Emotional Life.** Paul Ekman. Times Books, 2003.

GINA GORNY *Gehirn & Geist*

The pursuit of happiness drives much of what we do, but achieving it always seems just out of reach

Why It's So Hard to Be

HAPPY

By Michael Wiederman

What would make you happier? Perhaps a bigger house or a better car; a sexier or more understanding mate; surely, wealth and fame. Or maybe you would simply be happy with finishing everything on your to-do list. Well, stop deluding yourself. Psychological research suggests that none of these things is very likely to increase your happiness significantly.

PINK FRIDGE PRODUCTIONS *Getty Images*

Some people are naturally happier than others, thanks mainly to genetic differences. Happy people tend to be extroverted and to have a feeling of personal control over their lives.

Take money, for example. Using data from the 2000 U.S. Census, David G. Myers documented an interesting discrepancy between wealth and happiness. Myers, a psychologist at Hope College in Holland, Mich., found that the buying power of the average American had tripled since 1950. So were Americans three times happier in 2000 than 50 years earlier?

The National Opinion Research Center at the University of Chicago has asked Americans to rate their level of happiness in surveys that have been conducted most years since 1957. When Myers compared these surveys with the economic data, he found that the proportion of Americans who describe themselves as "very happy" has remained remarkably stable at about one third. Despite being far better off financially than previous generations, we are no happier.

In fact, young Americans are more anxious than in the past. In 2000 Jean M. Twenge, a psychologist now at San Diego State University, published a sweeping analysis of 269 studies conducted between 1952 and 1993—all of which had measured the anxiety levels of children or college students. When Twenge correlated the measurements with the dates of the studies, she found a strong linear increase in reported anxiety over time. The average American child in the 1980s reported more anxiety than child psychiatric patients of the 1950s.

Psychologists have long studied anxiety and depression, but in recent years they have also begun exploring the nature of what makes humans happy. The field of "positive psychology" is now a burgeoning one, and its results have led to some surprising conclusions. There is a growing body of evidence that happiness is not something that can be achieved by hard work or good luck. The happiest people seem to be those who are fully engaged in the present, rather than focused on future goals. What can we do to increase the likelihood of being happy? The answers may lie in our biological past.

Thanks for the Inheritance

When evolutionary psychologists notice a universal aspect of how people perceive the world, they make an assumption: that slice of human nature must have been adaptive for our distant ancestors. During our long evolutionary history, we passed certain characteristics to the next generation when the individuals who possessed them were more likely to survive and have offspring. Other ways of reacting to the world were weeded out, because the individuals who possessed brains wired to respond in those ways were less likely to survive or have offspring.

What does natural selection have to do with happiness? We humans have inherited a remarkable capacity to habituate to, or become accustomed to, the status quo. Habituation is wonderfully adaptive when we are faced with adverse conditions, such as chronic noise or a permanent disability. After a while, we may no longer even notice these unpleasant circumstances. Unfortunately, habituation applies to positive aspects of our lives as well. No matter how pleasant an experience is at first, if it becomes a constant, we habituate to it.

We have also inherited a tendency to notice the negative more readily than the positive. Those early *Homo sapiens* who were most sensitive to negative changes in the environment were probably most likely to survive, because negative changes may have signaled danger. Like our distant relatives, we, too, have brains that are wired to notice trouble. So the natural human condition is to take positive experiences for granted and to focus on the bothersome aspects of life.

Last, one other aspect of human nature helps to prevent us from being satisfied: that little voice inside our head that often convinces us that our life would be better if only we possessed or accomplished something else. It is easy to see how early humans who were never quite satisfied would have had an advantage over their more easily satisfied peers. That nagging voice of dissatisfaction would have prompted our ancestors to strive for a bit more and then a bit more after that.

Today we all share a certain set of human

How to Be Happier

① **DO NOT FOCUS ON GOALS.** Even though you may intellectually reject the idea that happiness can be achieved or bought, you must be constantly vigilant against that internal voice that whispers, "But I would be a bit happier if only ..." One strategy to try is to reflect on those times when you were convinced that a certain accomplishment or possession would bring greater happiness, yet your life was not significantly different after you reached your goal. How many times have you had this experience? How many more are needed to finally convince you that it does not work that way?

② **MAKE TIME TO VOLUNTEER.** People who volunteer to help those in need tend to report being happier. Perhaps it is because working with those less fortunate makes you grateful for what you have. Also, volunteering often brings satisfaction and self-esteem, because you feel engaged in worthwhile work and are appreciated by those you serve. Do not compare yourself with others who seem better off than you are, because that usually results in dissatisfaction.

③ **PRACTICE MODERATION.** If you grow too accustomed to pleasurable things, they will no longer bring you happiness. For example, you may enjoy two or three short vacations more than one long one. And you will enjoy your favorite meal more if you reserve it for a special occasion.

④ **STRIVE FOR CONTENTMENT.** Rethink your beliefs about the nature of happiness. Experiences of great pleasure or joy stand out in memory, and it is easy to conclude that being truly happy means being in that state most or all of the time. The very reason you savor and remember such an experience, however, is because it is not the norm. Instead of equating happiness with peak experiences, you would do better to think of happiness as a state of contentment and relative lack of anxiety or regret.

⑤ **PRACTICE LIVING IN THE MOMENT.** Start small by focusing on your sensory experience while engaged in a routine task. Over time, spend less energy thinking about the past or the future.

characteristics that prime us to be on a perpetual search for a better life. But that does not explain why some people seem to be happier than others. We might assume that happy people are those who have finally achieved the good life. Psychologists, however, have learned that happiness is more closely tied to personality than to life experiences.

The Power of Personality

Personality differs from human nature in that it varies across individuals. At the same time, personality is relatively stable across each person's lifetime. Events come and go, but our traits and habitual ways of responding remain.

When it comes to happiness, events influence how we feel, at least in the short run. Winning the lottery is liable to prompt even the most cynical individual to experience a sudden spike in happiness. Still, people habituate to the way things are and fall back to their personal baseline level of happiness. It is this inherent baseline, or set point, of happiness that is an aspect of personality. So why do different people have different set points for happiness?

A study of twins published in 1996 points to the answer. Researchers Auke Tellegen and the late David Lykken of the University of Minnesota compared the similarity in happiness scores among sets of identical and fraternal twins who grew up together or were reared apart. These comparisons enabled the researchers to determine the degree to which variations in happiness are related to variations in our genes. They found that about 80 percent of the variation in happiness among individuals was attributable to genetic differences.

When most people hear the word "genetic," they tend to think "passed from parents to offspring." In this case, however, "genetic" refers to a characteristic arising from the novel way genes come together to form each unique individual. This fact explains why traits that have a strong genetic component may still vary widely between parents and their children or between siblings. Unless an individual has an identical twin, that person is truly one of a kind genetically.

The notion that each of us has an inherent baseline of happiness—largely determined by our genes—has important implications when com-

Happy people tend to engage in activities that are challenging and absorbing. Such activities, dubbed "flow" experiences, force people to focus their full attention on the present moment.

GETTY IMAGES

bined with our shared human nature. The tendency to habituate to the status quo explains why, no matter what happens in our lives, we tend to return to our own individual set point of satisfaction with life.

Psychologists have discovered a number of personality traits that seem to be common in people with high set points of happiness. In a 1998 paper, social psychologist Kristina DeNeve of Baylor University (now at Creighton University) and psychologist Harris Cooper of the University of Missouri–Columbia (now at Duke University) reviewed 148 studies of the relation between personality and happiness. Perhaps not surprisingly, they found that people who reported being happier also reported being more extroverted, friendly, trusting and conscientious. Happier people were also more likely to believe they had control over their lives and were less prone to anxiety and mood swings.

The personality traits associated with happiness seem to be characteristics that are also related to personal success and achievement. Can happiness (or at least satisfaction) be won through hard work and determination? After all, isn't that the core belief underlying the American dream?

Goals + Achievement = Happiness?

American capitalism rests on the assumption that we can achieve or buy happiness, a belief that fuels competition and consumerism. The research showing a lack of correlation between wealth and happiness casts doubt on this assumption. But competing for wealth is more than just an unproductive way to achieve happiness; it is a recipe for unhappiness.

Psychologists refer to our tendency to compare ourselves with those who are better off as "upward comparison," and it is known to engender dissatisfaction. Using data from U.S. surveys conducted by the National Opinion Research Center between 1989 and 1996, Michael R. Hagerty of the Graduate School of Management at the University of California, Davis, studied the relation between happiness and the distribution of wealth in one's community. He found that the greater the income disparity within a community, the less its residents were satisfied with their lives. Analyzing data from the U.S. and seven other nations collected between 1972 and 1994, Hagerty found that as the inequality of income lessened within a particular country, the average level of life satisfaction increased.

It seems that when we are aware that others

are better off than we are, our own satisfaction suffers. Conversely, downward comparison (to those who are worse off than we are) tends to make us more appreciative and satisfied. The bad news? Upward comparison seems to come more naturally, a tendency that may be fueled by the mass media.

Even when we are not competing directly with others, our tendency to link happiness to the achievement of goals is counterproductive. Although more research is needed, psychologists William D. McIntosh of Georgia Southern University and Leonard L. Martin of the University of Georgia have theorized that people who re-

Trying to keep up with the Joneses? Psychologists warn against comparing yourself with others who are more fortunate.

(The Author)

MICHAEL WIEDERMAN is associate professor of psychology at Columbia College, an all-women's liberal arts college in South Carolina. He founded Mindful Publications, LLC (www.mindingthemind.com), a business that offers products and services that bridge the gap between psychology and individual consumers.

Success is related to happiness—but as a consequence, not a cause, of mood.

People who link happiness with goal achievement are setting themselves up for trouble. Unmet goals can cause anxiety, and fulfilled goals are quickly forgotten.

peatedly focus on attaining goals are less likely to be happy.

We might think of each person as falling somewhere along a continuum of linking happiness with goal attainment: from "nonlinker" to "strong linker." McIntosh and Martin say the problem with being a strong linker is the tendency to then be obsessively focused on meeting specific goals. Because of the belief that happiness depends on reaching those goals, strong linkers tend to experience anxiety and pressure as long as the goals remain unmet. They believe that happiness will be attained only at some future point. But what about when their goal is finally achieved?

After cherished goals are realized, habituation takes over, and strong linkers return to their previous baseline level of happiness just like everyone else. But when a strong linker realizes that his or her level of happiness has not permanently changed, the person typically concludes that happiness lies just over the next horizon.

Psychologists have found that we humans are good at deceiving ourselves about the future. We tend to believe that our prospects for increased happiness are better than our current circumstances. This tendency is nurtured by the media and advertising, which promise greater satisfaction with certain purchases or successes. People

who persist as strong linkers tend to choose new goals, convinced that this time they have found the "real" path to happiness.

The choice to continue to link happiness to achievement of goals may be bolstered by observation. Doesn't it seem that successful people are happier? Research supports such a connection, but not in the way we usually assume.

In 2005 Sonja Lyubomirsky, a psychologist at the University of California, Riverside, and her colleagues reviewed the results of studies showing a positive correlation between happiness and success. They also examined longitudinal studies—in which happiness was measured both before and after some specific success—as well as experiments in which pleasant, neutral or negative feelings were induced in participants before the start of some task. In both types of research, happiness and positive mood were important as precursors to success. Happy people were not necessarily happier after their success than they were before, but they tended to be happier than others who were less successful.

Lyubomirsky concluded that success is related to happiness—but as a consequence, not a cause, of mood. The most likely explanation is that happy people have other personality traits that facilitate success. Also, a positive mood is liable to result in greater motivation, as well as cooperation from others. But how can you achieve happiness (and the success that comes with it) if your personality is not naturally sunny?

Go with the Flow

Mihaly Csikszentmihalyi, a psychologist at Claremont Graduate University, has concluded that the people who tend to be happier are those who report experiencing what he calls "flow." Csikszentmihalyi coined the term in a 1975 book that was based on hundreds of interviews. He has since published several other books on flow, which he defines as experiences that are inherently interesting and motivating for an individual because he or she becomes totally absorbed in them. That is not to say that flow experiences have to be fun (although frequently they are) but rather that flow involves being fully engaged. The task at hand is not too boring or too frustrating; it is sufficiently challenging to require one's full attention.

ROBERT DECELIS Getty Images

KEN CHERNUS Getty Images

By incorporating the notion of flow, Western psychology has embraced the Eastern concept of mindfulness, which requires its practitioners to be nonjudgmental and conscious only of the present—immersed in what is happening right now. Unfortunately, this state of mind is not the norm for most of us; it is a skill that requires practice—through meditation, for example.

Why do people who report experiencing more flow also tend to be happier? Prominent psychologists, from Carl Rogers to Fritz Perls, describe psychological health as living in the present moment. Perhaps the link between happiness and flow has to do with the fact that flow experiences demand complete attention to the present. When we are totally engaged in what we are doing right now, it is impossible to focus on the past or future or to feel self-conscious—all of which tend to undermine satisfaction with life.

The growing body of research on happiness does not point to any easy answers. The roots of happiness are tangled, but understanding the inherent ways that our minds work does afford us the chance to make better choices about how we will invest our effort and time in the pursuit of happiness. Research from psychology seems to support what so many nonpsychologists have said before: happiness is not an ultimate destination but instead lies in appreciation of the journey. M

People who do volunteer work tend to be happier, perhaps because of "downward comparison" with others who are less fortunate.

(Further Reading)

◆ **Subjective Well-Being: Three Decades of Progress.** Ed Diener et al. in *Psychological Bulletin,* Vol. 125, No. 2, pages 276–302; 1999.
◆ **Authentic Happiness: Using the New Positive Psychology to Realize Your Potential for Lasting Fulfillment.** Martin Seligman. Free Press, 2004.
◆ **The Happiness Hypothesis.** Jonathan Haidt. Basic Books, 2005.
◆ **Happiness: The Science behind Your Smile.** Daniel Nettle. Oxford University Press, 2006.
◆ **Stumbling on Happiness.** Daniel Gilbert. Alfred A. Knopf, 2006.

In infants, **Elizabeth Spelke** finds fundamental insights into how men and women think
By David Dobbs

Big Answers from Little People

I f you had been blind all your life and could suddenly see, could you distinguish by sight what you knew already by touch—say, a cube from a sphere? Would flowers look like flowers you'd felt and faces like faces, or would they all be confusing patterns? How would you start to make sense of the many objects in your immediate view? If we are born knowing nothing, how do we come to know anything?

Harvard University psychologist Elizabeth Spelke takes these questions to the people who may be best able to answer them: babies. Spelke, whose sprawling laboratory in William James Hall teems with infants and researchers who are interested in them, has addressed some of the most intractable mysteries of human knowledge by interrogating little people who cannot yet talk, walk or even crawl. She has what she calls "an insatiable appetite" for assessing these young beings. Through Web pages, flyers and letters to day care centers and pediatricians' offices, her lab mates ask anyone and everyone for diminutive volunteers. They watch as the little subjects sit on their mothers' laps, tracking the stagecraft that Spelke and her cohorts use to gauge early understanding of numbers, language, objects, space and movement.

Spelke's findings have helped revise sharply our notion of what humans can make sense of in their first days, weeks and months. In doing so, she has offered some of the most substantial evidence to date regarding nature versus nurture and innate versus acquired traits. Spelke's discoveries about infant capabilities have become central to figuring out human cognition.

From her insights she has forged a bold, if still controversial, theory of "core knowledge," which asserts that all humans are born with basic cognitive skills that let them make sense of the world. This core knowledge, she says, underlies everything we learn throughout our lives and both unifies and distinguishes us as a species. Her theory prompted the American Psychological Association to honor her with its William James Fellow Award in 2000. And her work shows that, despite people's differences, we all have more in common than we recognize.

Clarity, Not Confusion

The heart of Spelke's methodology is her observation of "preferential looking"—the tendency of infants and children to peer longer at something that is new, surprising or different. Show a baby a toy bunny again and again, and the baby will give it a shorter gaze each time. But give the bunny four ears on, say, its tenth appearance, and if the baby looks longer, you know the baby

can discern four from two. The approach neatly bypasses infants' deficiencies in speech or directed movement and makes the most of the one thing they control well: how much time they fix their eyes on an object.

Spelke did not invent the scheme of studying preferential looking. That credit falls to Robert L. Fantz, a Western Reserve University psychologist who in the 1950s and early 1960s discovered that chimps and infants stare longer at things they perceive as unexpected. A researcher could gauge an infant's discriminatory and perceptual powers by showing the baby different, highly controlled scenarios, usually within a stagelike box, and observing what changes in the scenarios the infant would perceive as novel.

Using this basic technique, Fantz and others soon found that the infant's world was not, as pioneering psychologist William James had opined in 1890, a "blooming, buzzing confusion." Infants made sense of the world readily. For example, Fantz and others found that newborns could differentiate red from green, two-month-olds could discriminate all primary colors, and three-month-olds preferred yellow and red to blue and green. They found that a newborn could distinguish between her mother's face and a stranger's (unless both adults wore scarves over their hair), a four-

> ## Spelke has shown that humans of all races and both sexes are born with similar "core knowledge."

month-old could recognize acquaintances, and a six-month-old could interpret facial expressions. By the 1970s psychologists recognized the first year of life as a far more explosive developmental period than they had ever considered it to be.

This work attracted Spelke when she was still an undergraduate at Radcliffe College. From 1967 to 1971, she studied with Harvard child developmental psychologist Jerome Kagan and quickly found herself hooked on the excitement of investigating the essential workings of human cognition by analyzing children. She continued that research while pursuing her Ph.D. in psychology at Cornell University, where the famed developmental psychologist Eleanor J. Gibson served as her graduate adviser and mentor. Gibson, one of only a handful of psychologists to win the National Medal of Science, had revealed much about infant cognition with some elegant experiments of her own. Her best known was the "visual cliff,"

ROSE LINCOLN *Harvard News Office (preceding pages)*

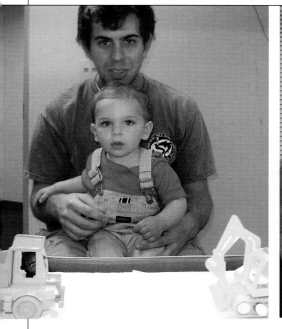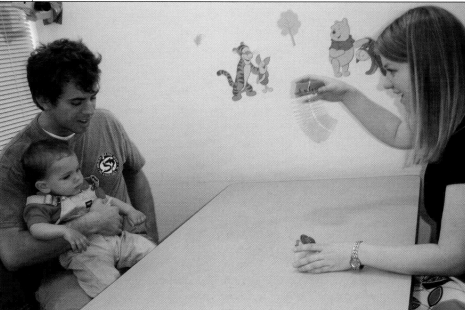

KATHARINA CIEPLAK-VON BALDEGG

a piece of heavy glass extending from a tabletop. Would early crawlers avoid the apparent drop-off? Most do, a discovery that revised theories of infants' spatial understanding.

Under such tutelage, Spelke hit on her own landmark experiment. "At dinner one night," she recalls as we talk in her office at Harvard, "I was musing with a fellow student over whether, when babies look at and listen to something, do they perceive [the sight and sound of an event] as two separate things, or do they recognize a link between the two? How would you find that out? Suddenly, I had this image of two visual events going on side by side, like movies, and between them a loudspeaker that you could switch from the sound of one event to the sound of the other event. Would a baby turn to look at the event matching the soundtrack the speaker was playing? That experiment became my Ph.D. thesis. It was the first time I was able to start with a general question about how we organize a unitary world from multiple modalities and turn the question into a ridiculously simple preferential-looking experiment—which actually ended up working."

Sure enough, Spelke found that babies recognized the link between sound and sight, switching their gaze back and forth as the soundtrack changed. Thus began Spelke's career of pondering big questions with straightforward experiments on tiny people. The mixed-modality approach addressed the same "binding problem" faced by blind people who suddenly can see: How does the brain mesh the signals from different senses into a single impression? Spelke did not

answer how, but she did show persuasively that this ability seems innate.

Native Knowledge

Over the years Spelke has conjured up many other elegant and productive investigations on object and facial recognition, motion, spatial navigation, and numerosity (grasping of numerical relationships). She is able to envision simple but powerful tests, she says, "because I think like a three-year-old." By showing babies objects in motion and then interrupting their logical speed or course, she has found that even a four-month-old infers that a moving object is supposed to keep moving. Yet it takes an eight-month-old to grasp the principle of inertia and expect the object's path to be consistent and smooth. By showing babies different arrays of disks, she has found that six-month-olds can distinguish eight from 16 and 16 from 32—but not eight from 12 or 16 from 24. By having babies watch a person reach for one of two objects on a table, she has found that although 12-month-olds know from an adult's gaze which object he will grab, eight-month-olds do not.

As the data from such clever designs mounted, Spelke began to develop her theory of core knowl-

Researchers gauge an infant's perceptual, attentional and discriminatory powers by manipulating objects in highly controlled scenarios and recording what the baby focuses on (*left*) and which changes he or she perceives as novel (*right*).

(The Author)

DAVID DOBBS profiled California Institute of Technology consciousness researcher Christof Koch in the most recent issue of *Scientific American Mind*. He is author of *Reef Madness: Charles Darwin, Alexander Agassiz, and the Meaning of Coral* (Pantheon Books, 2005). His writing can be found at www.daviddobbs.net

Spelke was plunged into controversy in 2005 when Harvard University president Lawrence Summers (*opposite page*) remarked that biology might explain why women occupy so few college math and science jobs. The foundations for these disciplines, she said publicly, "develop equally in males and females."

edge, often inspired by or collaborating with colleagues such as noted Massachusetts Institute of Technology linguist Noam Chomsky, French mathematician turned cognitive neuropsychologist Stanislaus Dehaene and Harvard psychologist Susan Carey. Core knowledge systems, Spelke says, are neuronal "modules" that are in place at birth for building mental representations of objects, persons, spatial relationships and numerosity. Somewhat akin to the "deep grammar" that Chomsky believes underlies all human language, these core knowledge modules enable all infants to organize their perceptions.

The sophistication of these systems in infants resembles that of modules in nonhuman primates, suggesting an ancient, evolutionary development; a six-month-old baby understands numbers, space, objects and faces much as a mature rhesus monkey does. As Spelke sees it, these cognitive tools underlie all the more complex skills and knowledge we master as we grow up—spoken languages, number manipulation and other abstract mental operations. Core knowledge forms the basis for the robust cognitive machinery that gets us

through life. And we almost completely ignore it.

"Even for adults," Spelke says, "most of what we know that lets us negotiate the world, guide our choice of paths through the environment, understand whether a car down the street might hit us or whether a falling object will miss us, even what we say as we're conversing—most of that is completely unconscious. How many things do we do that we hardly think about? Most of what we do is like that. We operate on richly structured cognitive systems that aren't usually accessible to introspection. To me, this is one more sign that most of our cognitive workings are much like those of babies and are built on the core knowledge that we had as babies."

Equality of the Sexes

This view of Spelke's is what philosophers call a "nativist" theory—that certain of our traits are inborn. They are natural rather than nurtured. Spelke knows well that this puts her on a slippery slope. To speak of native abilities is to court speculation about native differences in those abilities. In 2005, Spelke found herself involved in a hot controversy about such possible differences when she was repeatedly asked for her opinion of Harvard president Lawrence Summers's remarks that biological disparities might help explain why women occupy so few places in university math and science departments. Spelke, of course, was the natural choice to debate this topic, not only because she was a prominent, highly accomplished scientist at Summers's university but because she got there by studying precisely the innate abilities Summers wondered about. Although she hardly seems a scrapper by inclination, Spelke is quick-witted, funny, impressively well informed and eminently agile in conversation. And she rose quite gracefully to the task of popping Summers's thought balloon.

"If you look at things Summers's way," she says in her office, leaning forward in her chair with a sly grin, "then to study innate cognitive abilities, like I do, is supposedly to study gender differences. In fact, I didn't know we were studying gender differences at all, because we don't find any. But since the subject came up"—she spread her hands, clasped them, then sat back in her chair, smiling—"I was happy to tell him about our work."

Summers got an earful, if not directly, as Spel-

KIRSTEN CONDRY

After controversial remarks about women's abilities in math and science, Summers (*center*) announced that Harvard would spend $50 million to bolster female and minority faculty.

ke described in several interviews and in a high-profile public debate with her colleague and friend, Harvard psychologist Steven Pinker, how voluminous evidence from decades of research shows little if any inherently sex-based differences in infants or toddlers. At those early ages, when culture has the least effect but sex hormone levels are extremely high, no sex-based differences have shown themselves in a huge variety of skills that underlie mathematical thinking. For example: put a four-year-old in a distinctly shaped room, hide a block in a corner, have the four-year-old close his eyes and spin around, then have the child hunt for the block. Some of the children will quickly reorient themselves in the room and find the object, whereas others will not. Yet the percentages of boys and girls who succeed are identical. So although "there is a biological foundation to mathematical and scientific reasoning," as Spelke put it in her debate with Pinker, "these systems develop equally in males and females."

Spelke, an unabashed optimist, believes our growing understanding of cognitive abilities will eventually reduce, rather than inspire, divisions about our human qualities. "This idea that we have native abilities," she tells me, "some find threatening, for it seems to invite the idea that some types of people might be innately better endowed than others. If you're a nativist about basic core cognitive capacities, as I am, does that also lead you to be a nativist about, say, differ-ences among the sexes? These claims of biological bases can proliferate to a point where they end up being invoked to explain everything. But you have to be very careful about what data you use." The information that seems to indicate sex differences, Spelke says, comes from problematic studies whose results are colored by cultural influences—everything from parents responding differently to girls and boys to university faculties viewing identical job applications more skeptically when the applicant's name is female. Summers must have taken that last point to heart: in May he announced that Harvard would spend $50 million over 10 years to recruit and support women and minorities on its faculty.

Meanwhile the expanding pile of data on infants, who are not tainted by culture, shows remarkable parity among sexes and races. "We're getting evidence for an intricate and rich system of core knowledge that everyone shares and that gives us common ground," Spelke declares. "In a world of so much conflict, I think that's something we badly need." M

(Further Reading)

◆ **Test Subjects in Diapers.** Gisa Aschersleben in *Scientific American Mind,* Premier issue, Vol. 14, No. 5, pages 74–77; 2004.
◆ **Number Sense in Human Infants.** F. Xu, E. S. Spelke and S. Goddard in *Developmental Science,* Vol. 8, No. 1, pages 88–101; January 2005.
◆ **Pinker versus Spelke: A Debate.** Available on Edge: The Third Culture Web site: **www.edge.org/3rd_culture/debate05/debate05_index.html**

Set in Our Ways

in

Millions of us dream of transforming our lives, but few of us are able to make major changes after our 20s. Here's why

By Nikolas Westerhoff

"The shortest path to oneself leads around the world."

So wrote German philosopher Count Hermann Keyserling, who believed that travel was the best way to discover who you are.

That was how 22-year-old Christopher McCandless was thinking in the summer of 1990, when he decided to leave everything behind—including his family, friends and career plans. He gave his bank balance of $24,000 to the charity Oxfam International and hitchhiked around the country, ending up in Alaska. There he survived for about four months in the wilderness before dying of starvation in August 1992. His life became the subject of writer Jon Krakauer's 1996 book *Into the Wild*, which inspired the 2007 film of the same name.

Not every newly minted college graduate is as impulsive and restless as McCandless was, but studies conducted since the 1970s by personality researchers Paul Costa and Robert R. McCrae of the National Institutes of Health confirm that people tend to be open to new experiences during their teens and early 20s. Young people fantasize about becoming an adventurer like McCandless rather than following in the footsteps of a grandparent who spent decades working for the same company. But after a person's early 20s, the fascination with novelty declines, and resistance to change increases. As Costa and McCrae found, this pattern holds true regardless of cultural background.

Although people typically lose their appetite for novelty as they age, many continue to claim a passion for it. Voters cheer on politicians who pledge change. Dieters flock to nutritional programs advertising a dream figure in only five weeks. Consumers embrace self-help books promising personal transformation. And scientists tell us that novel stimuli are good for our brains, promoting learning and memory [see "Learning by Surprise," on page 71].

Yet even as people older than 30 yearn for what is new, many find themselves unable or unwilling to make fundamental changes in their lives. Researchers say this paradox can be largely explained by the demands of adult responsibilities and that unrealistic expectations may also play a part in thwarting our best intentions. Change is rarely as easy as we think it will be.

The Age of Openness

Psychologists have long identified openness to new experiences as one of the "Big Five" personality traits, which also include extroversion, agreeableness, conscientiousness and neuroticism. Considerable disagreement exists about how much these personality traits change after age 30, but most research suggests that openness declines in adulthood.

THE ROAD NOT TAKEN: For some, the long path to self-discovery begins with expanding one's geographic horizons.

CALL OF THE WILD: To fulfill a dream, 22-year-old Christopher McCandless hitchhiked across the U.S. in the 1990s, making his way to the Alaskan wilderness. His adventurous life was the subject of the film *Into the Wild,* starring Emile Hirsch.

VINCENT BESNAULT Getty Images (preceding pages); RIVER ROAD/PARAMOUNT/THE KOBAL COLLECTION (still from Into the Wild)

"Clear age trends are observable," says psychologist Peter Borkenau of Martin Luther University Halle-Wittenberg in Germany. "People tend to become more reliable and agreeable with age, but their openness to novelty drops at the same time."

In a comprehensive survey of more than 130,000 participants published in 2003, psychologist Sanjay Srivastava, now at the University of Oregon, and his colleagues assessed the Big Five traits in 21- to 60-year-olds using standard psychological tests on the Internet. They found that openness increased modestly up to age 30 and then declined slowly in both men and women. The survey results suggest that men begin adulthood slightly more open to new experiences than women but decline in openness during their 30s at a faster rate than women.

Age 30 is not a magical turning point, however. Openness declines gradually over many years, often beginning in the 20s. As the years wear on, novelty becomes less and less stimulating, and the world outside someone's own private and professional sanctums becomes increasingly less attractive.

This change happens to almost everyone, regardless of individual personality. That does not mean that everyone reaches the same level of openness in later life, however. Some toddlers love to go back to the same playground day after day, whereas others get bored after a day or two of digging in the same sandbox with the same shovel. Children who are less open to new experiences than their peers are will continue in adulthood to cleave to the conventional more than their more adventurous childhood friends will. As psychologist Richard W. Robins of the University of California, Davis, showed in a longitudinal study, those who begin life with a more open personality remain relatively more open in their later years.

Nature or Nurture?

The fact that an age-dependent pattern of decreasing openness appears around the globe and in all cultures suggests, according to biopsychologists, a genetic basis. But the jury is still out. As psychologist and personality researcher Rainer Riemann of Bielefeld University in Germany points out, it is conceivable that people all over the globe are simply confronted with similar life demands and societal

FAST FACTS
Personality through the Years

1 ›› Studies of personality development often focus on traits such as extroversion, conscientiousness, agreeableness, neuroticism and openness to new experiences. In most people, these traits change more during young adulthood than any other period of life, including adolescence. Openness typically increases during a person's 20s and goes into a gradual decline after that.

2 ›› This pattern of personality development seems to hold true across cultures. Although some see that as evidence that genes determine our personality, many researchers theorize that personality traits change during young adulthood because this is a time of life when people assume new roles: finding a partner, starting a family and beginning a career.

3 ›› Personality can continue to change somewhat in middle and old age, but openness to new experiences tends to decline gradually until about age 60. After that, some people become more open again, perhaps because their responsibilities for raising a family and earning a living have been lifted.

Learning by Surprise

Novelty enhances memory. That fact has practical implications for educators

By Daniela Fenker and Hartmut Schütze

You take the same route to work every day, driving the same car, crossing the same intersection with the same median strip. Same old, same old. But this morning something new catches your eye: a cow grazing in the median. It takes a couple of honks to remind you that the light has turned green.

If you are like most people, you will remember this moment in your morning commute for a long time—the sun was shining, daffodils had just pushed up in the median, and "We Are the Champions" was playing on the radio. Yet all the other countless times you have driven through this intersection are long forgotten.

Psychologists have known for some time that if we experience a novel situation within a familiar context, we will more easily store this event in memory. But only recently have studies of the brain begun to explain how this process happens and to suggest new ways of teaching that could improve learning and memory.

Novelty Detector

One of the most important brain regions involved in discovering, processing and storing new sensory impressions is the hippocampus, located in the temporal lobe of the cerebral cortex. Novel stimuli tend to activate the hippocampus more than familiar stimuli do, which is why the hippocampus serves as the brain's "novelty detector."

The hippocampus compares incoming sensory information with stored knowledge. If these differ, the hippocampus sends a pulse of the messenger substance dopamine to the substantia nigra (SN) and ventral tegmental area (VTA) in the midbrain. From there nerve fibers extend back to the hippocampus and trigger the release of more dopamine. Researchers, including John Lisman of Brandeis University and Anthony Grace of the University of Pittsburgh, call this feedback mechanism the hippocampal-SN/VTA loop (*above right*).

This feedback loop is why we remember things better in the context of novelty. As Shaomin Li and his colleagues at Trinity College Dublin discovered in 2003, the release of dopamine in the hippocampus of rats activates the synapses among nerve cells, creating stronger connections that lead to long-term memory storage. We wondered whether this same neuronal loop facilitates the retention of other information that is perceived along with novel stimuli.

At the University of Magdeburg's Institute for Cognitive Neurology, in collaboration with Emrah Düzel and Nico Bunzeck of University College London, we used functional magnetic resonance imaging to measure the activity of various brain regions based on blood flow. We presented one group of test subjects with a set of already known images and a second group with a combination of known and new images. Subjects in the second group were better at remembering the images than subjects in the first group were, and the fMRI data showed greater activity in the SN and VTA areas of the brain when the subjects were viewing unfamiliar images. This correlation may help explain how novelty improves memory.

Increased Retention

Are the effects of novelty on memory merely temporary? To answer this question, we showed test subjects a variety of photographs and measured their brain activity using fMRI. We also gave the participants a series of words to sort according to their meaning.

The experiment continued the next day when we showed some of the test subjects new images while others viewed familiar ones. Then we asked all the subjects to recall as many words from the previous day's exercise as they could. Recall was significantly better in the group that had just viewed new images.

In other words, novelty seems to promote memory. This finding gives teachers a potential tool for structuring their lessons more effectively. Although most teachers start a lesson by going over material from the previous class before moving on to new subject matter, they should probably do just the opposite: start with surprising new information and then review the older material.

Daniela Fenker and Hartmut Schütze are researchers at the University of Magdeburg's Neurology Clinic II in Germany.

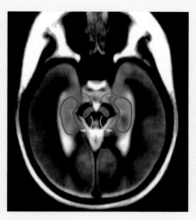

FEEDBACK LOOP: The hippocampus (*circled in blue in brain cross section*) responds to novel stimuli by sending a burst of the messenger substance dopamine (*red*) to the substantia nigra and the ventral tegmental area (SN/VTA; *circled in green*), according to the hippocampal-SN/VTA loop model. From the SN/VTA, nerve fibers run back to the hippocampus (*yellow*), triggering the release of additional dopamine in response to novelty. These brain structures deteriorate with age, which may help account for why seniors sometimes have trouble remembering new information.

The "Big Five" Personality Traits

In the 1970s two research teams led by Paul Costa and Robert R. McCrae of the National Institutes of Health and Warren Norman and Lewis Goldberg of the University of Michigan at Ann Arbor and the University of Oregon, respectively, discovered that most human character traits can be described using five dimensions. Surveys of thousands of people yielded these largely independent traits:

>> **Extroversion** The most broadly defined of the Big Five factors measures cheerfulness, initiative and communicativeness. Those who score high for extroversion are companionable, sociable and able to accomplish what they set out to do. Those with low scores tend to be introverted, reserved and more submissive to authority.

>> **Openness** People with high scores here love novelty and are generally creative. At the other end of the scale are those who are more conventional in their thinking, prefer routines, and have a pronounced sense of right and wrong.

>> **Agreeableness** This trait describes how we deal with others. High values show that someone is friendly, empathetic and warm. Shy, suspicious and egocentric individuals score low on the spectrum.

>> **Conscientiousness** This dimension measures a person's degree of organization. Those with high scores are motivated, disciplined and trustworthy. Irresponsible and easily distracted people are found at the low end of the scale.

>> **Neuroticism** This scale measures emotional stability. People with high scores are anxious, inhibited, moody and less self-assured. Those at the lower end are calm, confident and contented.

Where are you on the Big Five scale? You can find out by taking a free personality test at **www.outofservice.com/bigfive** —N.W.

expectations. Young men and women everywhere have to go out into the world and find a partner and a livelihood. Later, they have to care for their children and grandchildren. These life tasks require commitment and consistency and may serve as a catalyst for personality change.

Once a family and career are in place, novelty may no longer be as welcome. New experiences may bring innovation and awakening but also chaos and insecurity. And so most people dream of novelty but hold fast to the familiar. Over time we become creatures of habit: enjoying the same dishes when we eat out, vacationing in favorite spots and falling into daily routines.

"The brain is always trying to automate things and to create habits, which it imbues with feelings of pleasure. Holding to the tried and true gives us a feeling of security, safety, and competence while at the same time reducing our fear of the future and of failure," writes brain researcher Gerhard Roth of the University of Bremen in Germany in his 2007 book whose title translates as *Personality, Decision, and Behavior.*

But even negative events may have thoroughly positive results, according to sociologist Deborah Carr of Rutgers University. For example, many widows are able to start life over again and to develop talents they never knew they had. People who have been diagnosed with cancer learn to redefine themselves as a result of the disease—and may even conquer their cancer in the process. Survivors of natural catastrophes often discover new strengths. But we should not draw sweeping conclusions from these examples, says psychologist William R. Miller of the University of New Mexico. Many older people report that they have changed little in spite of major life experiences.

In a recent experiment psychologist Kate C. McLean of the University of Toronto Mississauga asked 134 volunteers of different ages—some older than 65 and others ranging in age from late adolescence through young adulthood—to describe three self-defining memories. She found that both old and young participants reported novel experiences such as the death of a partner, an unexpected career advancement or a cross-country move. The older people ascribed different meanings to these events than the younger people did, however. For younger people, external changes were more likely to lead to internal transformation, but that was not the case for older individuals.

These very different narratives are no coinci-

(The Author)

NIKOLAS WESTERHOFF has a doctorate in psychology and is a science journalist in Berlin.

dence. Personality traits change more during young adulthood than any other period of life, according to psychologist Brent W. Roberts of the University of Illinois, who together with two colleagues analyzed 92 studies of personality development. They concluded that some personality changes occur well past the age of 30 but that typically these changes are small in magnitude compared with the changes that occur between the ages of 20 and 40.

Even major life events such as a divorce or the death of a loved one, though stressful, are unlikely to result in profound personality changes. The middle years of life are often a time of reflection and reevaluation, but few people experience a genuine "midlife crisis."

The structure of one's personality becomes increasingly stable until about age 60. "That means that a person who is particularly conscientious at the age of 40 will be conscientious at 60 as well," Borkenau says. Stability decreases again, however, after the age of 60. It seems that people are only able to become more open to new experiences once they have fulfilled their life obligations—that is, after they have retired from their careers and their children have flown the nest.

False Hope Springs Eternal

Even after age 60 it is difficult to completely reframe your life. In fact, those who seek to make large changes often end up failing even to make the most minor corrections. The more an individual believes he can set his own rudder as he pleases, the more likely he is to run aground. That's one reason why so many smokers who tell you that they can quit whenever they want are still smoking 20 years later.

In 1999 psychologists Janet Polivy and C. Peter Herman of the University of Toronto Mississauga coined a term for this phenomenon: false hope syndrome. Over and over, they say, people undertake both small and large changes in their lives. Most of these attempts never get anywhere, thanks to overblown expectations [see "Picture Imperfect," by David Dunning, Chip Heath and Jerry M. Suls; SCIENTIFIC AMERICAN MIND, Vol. 16, No. 4, 2005].

Take the woman who believes that if she can lose 20 pounds she will finally meet the man of her dreams and live happily ever after. This fantasy is based on the notion that one positive change—losing weight—automatically brings with it other desired changes. But the reality is that it is difficult to keep weight off over the long term, and finding an ideal life partner is often dependent on luck. Even if dieting proves successful, other goals may remain

HIGH FLIERS: Paragliding, parachuting and bungee jumping are a welcome change from the daily routine for some—for others, a nightmare.

out of reach. But the false hope syndrome seduces people into trying to overhaul their entire lives all at once: the smoker and couch potato is suddenly inspired to become a nonsmoker and marathon runner, but because he attempts too much too fast, he is doomed to fail.

The cure for false hope is to set more reasonable goals and recognize that achieving even modest change will be difficult. And if you are older than 30, remember that your openness to new experiences is slowly declining, so you are better off making a new start today than postponing it until later. Perhaps most important of all, try to appreciate the person that you already are.

As the ancient Greek philosopher Epicurus put it: "Do not spoil what you have by desiring what you have not; but remember that what you now have was once among the things only hoped for." M

(Further Reading)

◆ **Into the Wild.** Jon Krakauer. Villard Books, 1996.
◆ **Personality at Midlife: Stability, Intrinsic Maturation, and Response to Life Events.** Paul T. Costa, Jr., Jeffrey H. Herbst, Robert R. McCrae and Ilene C. Siegler in *Assessment,* Vol. 7, No. 4, pages 365–378; December 2000.
◆ **Development of Personality in Early and Middle Adulthood: Set Like Plaster or Persistent Change?** Sanjay Srivastava, Oliver P. John, Samuel D. Gosling and Jeff Potter in *Journal of Personality and Social Psychology,* Vol. 84, No. 5, pages 1041–1053; 2003.
◆ **Patterns of Mean-Level Change in Personality Traits across the Life Course: A Meta-analysis of Longitudinal Studies.** Brent W. Roberts, Kate E. Walton and Wolfgang Viechtbauer in *Psychological Bulletin,* Vol. 132, No. 1, pages 1–25; January 2006.
◆ **Stories of the Young and the Old: Personal Continuity and Narrative Identity.** Kate C. McLean in *Developmental Psychology,* Vol. 44, No. 1, pages 254–264; January 2008.

Neurotic about Neurons

Scientists today are using the latest imaging technologies to investigate Sigmund Freud's most fundamental tenets: that dreams represent unfulfilled wishes, that the three parts of the psyche—the ego, id and superego—have neuronal bases, and that "talk therapy" changes the physical networks of neurons in the brain. The fact that such work is happening at all represents an apparent comeback for psychoanalysis. No one would be happier than Freud himself. Although his followers like to think of his work as pure psychology, the young Freud built his theories on his own detailed investigation of animal and human brains. To him, every mental illness stemmed from a physical defect in the brain.

GETTY IMAGES

Freud's theories sprang directly from neuroscience, until he began interrogating sexually frustrated women
By Steve Ayan

His point of view changed, however, when he began treating women who were diagnosed as being "hysterical." They suffered from what appeared to be suppressed sexual desires. These cases and others prompted him to discard his own model of the brain as a kind of neuronal machine and replace it with a model of the mind as an entity driven by secret desires. Freud constructed his fantastic theories of dreaming, repression, and ego and id based on years of listening to troubled patients tell of their woes while lying on his office couch—a career move from the brain lab motivated primarily by Freud's need to make enough money to support his rapidly expanding family. And yet in his final writings, he acknowledged his own repressed hope that one day science would recast his maxims in neurology.

Rooted in Biology

Sigismund Schlomo Freud came into the world on May 6, 1856, as the first of eight children. He was born in Freiberg in the Austro-Hungarian Empire—today the town of Pribor in the Czech Republic. Four years later his mother and father, a wool dealer, moved the family to Vienna for good. The wool business never went well, and like most Eastern European Jewish immigrants the family struggled against anti-Semitism and poverty. Yet the Freuds set great hopes on their firstborn and nurtured his ambitions.

Young Freud, called Sigmund for short, enrolled as a medical student at the University of Vienna in 1873. The place had some of the finest minds in medical education. Among Freud's teachers was Ernst Brücke, a prominent physiologist, and at age 20 Freud entered his lab as an assistant, dedicated to studying the nervous systems of lower animals. His early publications included titles such as "On the Origin of the Posterior Nerve Roots in the Spinal Cord of Ammocoetes."

Neurophysiological research was a new but rising discipline. Brücke was a member of the Berlin Physical Society, whose motto was, "We have pledged ourselves to make this truth known: that within the organism no other forces are at work beyond normal physical-chemical ones." Freud, armed with a dissection knife and a microscope, strived to inform this strictly biological model.

In the summer of 1882—a year after receiving his degree—Freud was engaged to Martha Bernays, who came from a prominent family. The gifted but penniless physician now urgently needed money and status before he could marry Bernays, five years his junior. He wanted to continue in research but saw no prospects for rapid promotion in the university. So that same year he took a position at Vienna General Hospital, where over the next three years he would make rounds in all the important departments, including surgery, internal medicine and psychiatry.

1856
On May 6 Sigismund
Schlomo Freud is born
in Freiberg, Moravia (today
Pribor). In 1860 the family
moves to Vienna

Freud's birth house

The 16-year-old with
his mother

1867 ·----------
Karl Marx's *Das Kapital*
is published

1875 ·----------
Wilhelm Wundt begins
teaching at the University
of Leipzig in Germany,
where four years later he
will establish the first
psychological institute in
the world

1873 ·----------
In the fall the young Freud
begins his medical studies
at the University of Vienna
in Austria. After an unusu-
ally long time—eight years
as a student—he receives
his medical degree, at
the age of 25

1856   1867   1873   187?

The psychiatry department was headed by Theodor Meynert, a world-renowned brain researcher and a proponent of the idea of cerebral localization. This school of thought, much in vogue at the time, held that every psychopathological symptom—whether a speech defect, hallucination or mental illness—originated from a physical defect in the brain. An investigator's most important task was to locate such defects during autopsies. Meynert was convinced that psychiatric illness could be traced back to neuronal sources. He was suspicious of any patient's complaint that lacked a recognizable, organic cause; without such evidence, a patient's claim must simply spring from imagination or even be deliberately feigned.

Talk Therapy Begins

During his years with Meynert, Freud became an expert in cerebral localization. But soon his career would take a completely different path. Thanks to a traveling fellowship from his department, he left Vienna in 1885 to spend six months at the Salpêtrière hospital in Paris, where psychiatrist Jean-Martin Charcot was searching for a therapy for a disorder common among women: so-called hysteria.

The victims of hysteria suffered from sudden attacks of paralysis and aphasia (inability to comprehend speech). Some of them babbled as if delirious or became highly aroused sexually. The cause of this odd disorder was obscure, and the usual treatments—hydrotherapy or massage—seldom helped. So the charismatic Charcot hypnotized his patients and suggested to them that

they were, right then and there, experiencing the symptoms. Often the patients acted "hysterical," but once they were awakened from hypnosis they reported feeling improved. Freud was so caught up in Charcot's enthusiasm that he would later name his first son after the French doctor.

As soon as Freud returned to Vienna, he married Bernays, and the couple had six children in rapid succession. To earn enough to feed his growing family, Freud gave up research to become a neurologist in private practice. In 1891 the clan moved to larger quarters in Vienna—a house big enough to accommodate a room to treat patients. They stayed there for almost 50 years, until they had to flee the Nazis in 1938.

Soon after the move Freud furthered his relationship with Joseph Breuer, a physician who was experimenting with hypnosis as treatment for various mental ills. In 1895 the two jointly published *Studies on Hysteria*. This classic book of case studies marked the birth of psychoanalysis. The two doctors explained that hysterical women suffered, above all, from "reminiscences"—fragmentary memories of traumatic events such as sexual abuse—that broke into their conscious minds in the form of anxiety fantasies. This experiential, unconscious process contradicted the then dominant localization theory that every mental illness was traceable to a physical origin.

Freud developed the technique of "free association" as a means to gain access to the repressed memories of hysterical people and of those who exhibited compulsive behavior. Because the content of these memories was generally "hidden" in the unconscious and repressed from breaking

MARY EVANS PICTURE LIBRARY/SIGMUND FREUD COPYRIGHTS

A contemporary painting shows Jean-Martin Charcot hypnotizing a young woman

The famous couch, now a museum exhibit

The bride, Martha

1885

At the Salpêtrière hospital in Paris, Freud gets to know Jean-Martin Charcot, the French psychiatrist. Charcot's hypnosis of frantic female patients awakens Freud's interest in hysteria and ways to treat it

1879

Albert Einstein is born in Ulm, Germany

1886

Freud marries Martha Bernays. Over the next 10 years she will bear six children

1891

Freud moves his family to a larger home in Vienna, at street address Berggasse 19. Freud lives and works there for 47 years, until he and his family flee the Nazis

1895

Together with Joseph Breuer, Freud publishes *Studies on Hysteria*. The case studies in this collection form the cornerstone of psychoanalysis as a treatment method for mental ills

1899

In November, Freud's now famous *The Interpretation of Dreams* appears. The title page shows the date as 1900 to emphasize its historical significance

1879   1885 1886   1891   1895   1899

through to the patients' conscious awareness, Freud told his patients to relax on his couch and challenged them to tell him whatever came into their heads. The analyst noted everyday experiences, dreams and feelings. Even his patients' jokes and casual remarks were sources that could unveil the dramas of the unconscious mind. Freud's postulate was that bringing a neurotic disturbance into conscious discussion through therapy would cause the troubling notion to dissolve, by way of a mechanism he called the "cathartic" effect of psychoanalysis.

Freud's heart was not in treating patients, however. The tedious therapy sessions served above all as a laboratory for the refinement of his theories. Freud readily took the knowledge he obtained and applied it to people in general. As he wrote: "What analytic research originally had in mind was no more than finding the causes of a few pathological mental conditions, but in achieving this we were able to discover relationships of fundamental significance, and thus create a new psychology."

In 1899 Freud laid the foundations of psychoanalytic theory in his book *The Interpretation of Dreams*. The script presented a set of ideas that has influenced modern thought just as strongly as has Darwin's theory of evolution or Einstein's theory of relativity. In later decades Freud would revise, expand and even discard individual ideas within the theory; after World War I he postulated a second source of psychic energy—in addition to the libido—that he called Thanatos, or the "death instinct." The division of the psyche into three interactive parts—the driven id, the

moralistic superego and the ego that negotiated between the two—was chiefly delineated in the 1920s. But psychoanalysis persevered.

Dreams marked a complete turn away from neurology, treading purely in psychology. In it, Freud wrote, "We shall wholly ignore the fact that the psychic apparatus concerned is known to us also as an anatomical preparation, and we shall carefully avoid the temptation to determine the psychic locality in any anatomical sense. We shall remain on psychological ground." This position affected not just therapy but research methodology. The interpretation of reported dreams, for instance, had nothing in common with the search for brain injuries or arousal of the central nervous system.

Nevertheless, when it came to the "psychic apparatus," Freud continued, as before, to see both psychological and biological principles at work. This conundrum led him to the heart of the ancient mind-body problem—whether the mind is purely the outcome of neurons firing throughout the nervous system or whether it arises as a higher state. Freud had already imagined resolving it in 1895, when he drafted a report called *Project for a Scientific Psychology*. "The intention," he wrote, "is to furnish a psychology that shall be a natural science: that is, to represent psychic processes as quantitatively determinate states of specifiable material particles, thus making

(The Author)

STEVE AYAN has a degree in psychology and is an editor at *Gehirn & Geist*.

The secret "Committee," which set itself the goal of maintaining a pure doctrine of psychology unencumbered by physical brain considerations. From left: Otto Rank, Freud, Karl Abraham, Max Eitington, Sándor Ferenczi, Ernest Jones and Hanns Sachs

C. G. Jung, circa 1904

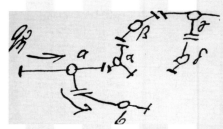

Diagram penned by Freud shows how he thought neurons repressed the flow of memories

1902
The first regular meetings of the Wednesday Psychoanalytic Society begin in Freud's home on Berggasse. From this circle of students, the Vienna Psychoanalytic Society arose in 1908. The first president of the International Psychoanalytic Association, founded in 1910, was C. G. Jung, a doctor from Zurich

1909
Together with Jung and Ferenczi, Freud travels to the U.S., where his talks about psychoanalysis arouse great interest

1913
Freud breaks ranks with Jung, his one-time "crown prince"

1914
World War I begins after the assassination of Archduke Franz Ferdinand, heir to the Austro-Hungarian throne, in Sarajevo

1923
Freud publishes *The Ego and the Id*. The ego mediates between the primal, driven id and the moralistic superego

1902   1909   1913 1914   1923

those processes perspicuous and free from contradiction." The "material particles" were most likely neurons, which were in contact with one another via synapses. What Freud meant by "quantities" was the level of psychic energy flowing through the neurons. The energy arose from arousal either by a sensory organ or—far more important—by the body's own drives. Discharging this energy—in the sex act, for instance—creates pleasure for the individual, whereas blocking its discharge creates displeasure.

Even this terse description makes it clear that Freud's metaphor for the organ of the mind was an electric motor. His psychodynamic model resembles an internal relay station that directs constantly flowing "current" into a complex, highly branched system. Occasionally, in some unknown way, this current quantity was transformed into quality—conscious experience. "Every psychic act begins as an unconscious one," Freud declared in his draft report.

Conflicted

Despite seemingly certain statements, Freud struggled mightily with whether to place his faith in biology or psychology. While working on *Project for a Scientific Psychology* in October 1895, he wrote to his friend Wilhelm Fliess in Berlin: "Everything fell into place, the cogs meshed, and the thing really seemed to be a machine which in a moment would run of itself." Yet just five weeks later he admitted his disappointment: "I no longer understand the state of mind in which I concocted this psychology." At the end, Freud discarded his plan for a neuronal machine, and the unfinished *Project* manuscript disappeared into a drawer.

Freud failed to reconcile the brain and mind because he saw no possibility of finding a neurological basis for distinguishing between conscious and unconscious processes—the magical hub around which his entire psychology revolved. The dead end is not surprising, given that research into brain function was still primitive. No one knew how the brain worked. Wilhelm Waldeyer had just introduced the concept of the neuron in 1891. The big question was whether the dense tissue of the brain was a single, spongelike mass, as Italian physician Camillo Golgi believed, or whether it was made of many tiny units, the concept favored by Spanish histologist Santiago Ramón y Cajal. Golgi developed a staining method that allowed scientists to study thin sections of brain under a microscope. Using it, Ramón y Cajal was able to identify narrow gaps between neuron cell bodies, leading him to the image of a myriad of intercommunicating units in the brain. This advancement brought Golgi and Ramón y Cajal the Nobel Prize in Physiology or Medicine in 1906.

Scientists were also largely in the dark about anatomical brain function. It had been 20 years since losses in certain regions of the mysterious gray organ had been linked to specific pathological symptoms. Paul Broca, a French neuroanatomist, investigated an aphasic who had unusual speech problems. The patient understood most of what was said to him yet could not produce a single intelligible sentence. After the patient died, Broca autopsied his brain and discovered lesions in a part of the left frontal lobe, known today as Broca's area; the ability to produce speech is lo-

Many Austrians hail the union with Nazi Germany in 1938

1938
In March the Wehrmacht marches into Vienna. In June the Freuds flee the city to London via Paris

On the train to Paris, with daughter Anna, in 1938

1930
Freud receives the Goethe Prize, the highest literary award of the Weimar Republic, for his life's work. His mother, Amalia, dies the same year

1933
The National Socialists take power in Germany

1939
Assisted suicide: Freud dies on September 23 of an overdose of morphine, injected by his physician Max Schur at Freud's request. Freud had suffered for many years from exceptionally painful cancer of the jaw

SIGMVND FREVD
6.5.1856–23.9.1939

Freud's burial urn in London

1930   1933   1938 1939

cated there. Broca's German colleague, Carl Wernicke, discovered the neurological seat of speech understanding—a part of the frontal lobe far above Broca's area; a patient with damage there cannot understand even the simplest speech but can still produce grammatically correct, though often meaningless, sentences.

Few other anatomical associations had been found by 1895, however. Physicians hoped every one of the gyri and sulci—the characteristic hills and valleys of the cerebral cortex—might be charted according to its function, but Freud was skeptical. What would that say about the psychic events taking place within them? His answer: Nothing. "We know two things concerning what we call our psyche or mental life: firstly, its bodily organ and scene of action, the brain (or nervous system) and secondly, our acts of consciousness, which are immediate data and cannot be more fully explained by any kind of description. Everything that lies between these terminal points is unknown to us, and, so far as we are aware, there is no direct relation between them. If it existed, it would at the most afford an exact localization of the processes of consciousness and would give us no help toward understanding them."

These words are found in the opening of *An Outline of Psychoanalysis*, Freud's last work, which he began shortly before his death in 1939. Here again Freud collected the most important points of his psychology. "The phenomena with which we have had to deal do not belong to psychology alone; they have an organic and biological side as well.... We have adopted the hypothesis of a psychic apparatus extended in space, appropriately constructed, developed by the exigencies of life, which gives rise to the phenomena of consciousness only at one particular point and under certain conditions. This hypothesis has put us in a position to establish psychology on foundations similar to those of any other science."

Was Freud's flirtation with biology no more than a "self-misunderstanding," as philosopher Jürgen Habermas wrote? Or did it merely serve as a pretext he used to endow his teachings with the prestige of science? There is a great deal of evidence that Freud did believe that psychoanalysis would, one day, have empirical foundations.

Some experts today are indeed attempting to lay the groundwork of "neuropsychoanalysis." Modern neuroscience, they claim, possesses the necessary methods and findings to support Freud's assumptions. Yet Freud himself realized that the converse might be true: "Biology is truly a land of unlimited possibilities. We may expect it to give us the most surprising information, and we cannot guess what answers it will return in a few dozen years to the questions we have put to it. They may be of a kind that will blow away the whole of our artificial structure of hypothesis." M

(Further Reading)

◆ **Freud, Biologist of the Mind: Beyond the Psychoanalytic Legend.** Frank J. Sulloway. Harvard University Press, 1992.

◆ **Freud's Requiem: Mourning, Memory, and the Invisible History of a Summer Walk.** Matthew Von Unwerth. Riverhead, 2005.

◆ **Complete Bibliography of Psychoanalysis and Neuroscience (1895–1999).** International Neuro-Psychoanalysis Society. Available for download at www.neuro-psa.org.uk/npsa/index.php?module=pagemaster&PAGE_user_op=view_page&PAGE_id=7

A growing body of research shows that groups can systematically enhance their performance

The Science of Team Success

By Steve W. J. Kozlowski and Daniel R. Ilgen

The right stuff: The dramatic rescue of *Apollo 13*'s astronauts would have been impossible without the coordinated efforts of NASA engineers. Research is revealing why some groups work so well together.

"Houston, we've had a problem," were the famous words that announced a crisis onboard *Apollo 13*. Halfway through *Apollo*'s mission to the moon, one of the spacecraft's oxygen tanks exploded, putting the lives of the crew in grave jeopardy. A group of engineers from NASA was hastily assembled. Their mission: invent a way for the crew to survive and to pilot their damaged vessel back to Earth. The engineers were successful, transforming a potential disaster into a legend of effective teamwork.

As experienced members leave and new people join a group, crucial bits of collective knowledge can be lost.

Human history is largely the story of people working together in groups to explore, achieve and conquer—and in our modern world the role of teams is only growing, spurred by globalization and the enabling factor of communications technology. Teams do not always play the role of hero, however. They have also been implicated in many political and military catastrophes, including the U.S. government's sluggish response to Hurricane Katrina, the failure to prevent the tragedy of 9/11 and the explosion of NASA's space shuttle *Columbia*.

Given the centrality of work teams, it is more than a bit remarkable how much our society's perspective is focused on the individual. We school our children as individuals. We hire, train and reward employees as individuals. Yet we have great faith that individuals thrown into a team that has been put together with little thought devoted to its composition, training, development and leadership will be effective and successful. Science strongly suggests otherwise.

We recently reviewed the past 50 years of research literature on teams and identified factors that characterize the best collaborations. It turns out that what team members *think*, *feel* and *do* provide strong predictors of team success—and these factors also suggest ways to design, train and lead teams to help them work even better.

Unfortunately, although society places a great value on teamwork, the way organizations make use of teams often runs against known evidence for what works—and even against common sense. For example, it seems obvious that teams need sufficient resources to enable members to accomplish their goals. Still, in this era of down-

FAST FACTS
Building Better Teams

1» An effective work group should be designed well from the start, bringing together people who can contribute to the right mix of knowledge, skills, tools and other resources necessary to succeed.

2» Face-to-face meetings, social interaction among members and a leader who establishes a good relationship with every worker help a team make the best use of its expertise and create a cohesive mission.

3» Generic teamwork skills such as setting goals, adapting to change, resolving conflict and providing feedback allow teams to learn from each challenge and continually improve their performance.

DAVID TROOD Getty Images

Organizations reward individuals based on individual performance rather than team performance.

sizing and cutbacks, one has to question the wisdom of many managers who believe that more can *always* be accomplished with less.

Consider, too, that organizations typically reward people with salaries, bonuses and promotions based on individual performance rather than team performance. These rewards can often inhibit team members' willingness to work together and help one another, even when the success of the team depends on it. Such success requires a delicate balance between meeting the goals of the team as well as those of the individuals who populate it. Research on goal setting, cooperation, competition, conflict and negotiation contributes to a better understanding of how people remain in teams and work together.

Indeed, a crucial question that should be asked before putting a team together is whether you need one at all. Some businesses recognize the importance of teams and promptly restructure every task so that it becomes a group respon-

sibility, even when the assignment is something that could be done easily by an individual working independently. The result is a team that is more likely to impede performance than enhance it. Another question is, What type of team structure is required? The task of some teams is such that their employees can function independently for long stretches and occasionally confer and pool their results, as with a team of salespeople working in different geographic regions. Others, such as surgical teams, require a high and constant degree of coordination.

The job assigned to a team also determines the primary focus of activities, and how well the individual members complete their related duties determines the team's efficiency. That is why team studies have turned to an approach known as organizational psychology, which focuses on the task as central to understanding the dynamics of teamwork and team performance. (In contrast, a traditional social psychology perspective

An effective group brings together people with the necessary knowledge, skills and tools to do the job.

focuses more on interactions among peers, and the work merely serves as the context for those exchanges.) As mentioned before, the task sets minimum requirements for the resource pool—the constellation of knowledge, skills, abilities and other characteristics (such as personality, values)—that is available across team members.

The Collective Mind

One of the most important things a team brings to a task is what its members *think*, the relevant information they carry in their heads. This knowledge can include a mastery of the tools they use and an understanding of the task at hand, its goals, performance requirements and problems. Some knowledge may be shared by all workers, whereas particular members might have specialized skills or know-how. The ability to access and use this distributed expertise efficiently is one characteristic of successful teams.

A 1995 experiment by psychologist Diane Wei Liang, then at the University of Minnesota, psychologist Richard L. Moreland of the University of Pittsburgh and Linda Argote, professor of organizational behavior and theory at Carnegie

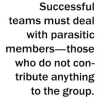

Successful teams must deal with parasitic members—those who do not contribute anything to the group.

Mellon University, nicely demonstrated how team members benefit from their collective knowledge when they learn together. These researchers trained college students to assemble transistor radios either alone or in groups of three. A week later the subjects were tested with their original group or, for people who received solo training, in newly formed groups. Members of groups that had trained together remembered more details, built better-quality radios and showed greater trust in fellow members' expertise. People in newly formed groups were less likely to have the right mix of skills to complete the task efficiently and knew less about one another's strengths.

With a different group of collaborators, Argote studied the effect of individual turnover on another chore, making origami birds. Again, groups of three trained together and were given six time periods to make as many paper products as possible. The groups with turnover produced significantly fewer folded creations than groups whose members stayed constant, suggesting aspects of group knowledge were being lost when people were replaced.

In an interesting twist, organizational behav-

RANDY FARIS *Corbis*

ior expert Kyle Lewis of the McCombs School of Business at the University of Texas at Austin found that the development of a team's ability to access distributed knowledge required face-to-face interaction. In groups that communicated exclusively by phone or e-mail, this skill did not emerge—an observation of increasing importance, given the rise of teams that operate remotely and coordinate sometimes only through computer interactions. It should prompt concerted efforts to understand the

less is understood about how emotional state affects team performance than about cognitive influences, it is clear that how teams feel can drag down productivity or boost it up—or otherwise complicate it. For example, a shared positive attitude can reduce the number of absences in teams and lower the likelihood that people will leave the group.

But there are hints that good moods do not always lead to good outcomes. Social psycholo-

One person's behavior leads to group-level changes in emotion, both negatively and positively.

reasons for such barriers and explore whether webcams, videoconferencing or other technologies that allow people to interact will help overcome this problem. For now, the best solution may be to guarantee some face time for team members throughout their project.

Beyond an understanding of the nuts and bolts of any given project, another cognitive influence on team effectiveness is the emergence of an overall objective, mission or strategic imperative of the group—something psychologists call the team climate. The powerful effect of climate on the real-world impact of teams is well established. For example, one of our groups (Kozlowski's) showed that high-tech businesses whose engineers agreed on the objective to stay technologically up-to-date showed improved performance and had more employees pursuing continuing education and displaying positive job attitudes. Several studies across many industries have shown that when a team has absorbed a mission statement that values customer service, this attribute predicts customer satisfaction. Likewise, when a team agrees that the objective is safety, the result is more safety-conscious behavior by team members and a reduction in the rate of accidents.

Ties That Bind

Climate emerges in groups with strong ties among their members. For example, team members who have a good relationship with their leader tend to share climate perceptions with their boss and co-workers. Teams that have frequent informal social interactions also show greater consensus on climate than those that do not.

Part of the glue that binds people to their bosses or to one another is emotional. Although

gist Joseph P. Forgas of the University of New South Wales in Australia, for example, asked teams to hold a discussion after they watched happy or sad videos and found that greater divisions arose in the groups that were given a prior "feel good" stimulus.

It also appears that team members tend to change their moods in concert. Social psychologist Peter Totterdell of the University of Sheffield in England and his colleagues had nurses record their moods each day at work over a period of three weeks. They found that the mood of different teams shifted together over time. Totterdell has measured a similar convergence in the affect of teams of accountants and cricket players.

The fact that emotions move in this lockstep way has led to a concept of emotional contagion, the idea that emotions within teams are transferred from one person to others close by. In a well-controlled laboratory study, professor of management Sigal Barsade of the Wharton School of the University of Pennsylvania investigated the effect of emotional contagion on team process and performance. The research involved using a drama student posing as a research subject whom Barsade trained to participate with a happy, optimistic attitude or an unpleasant, pessimistic one. She found that this one person's behavior did lead to group-level changes in emotion, both for positive and negative affect. Although the scientific study of how mood influences performance of the individual and the team as a whole is still in its infancy, this area promises to yield important insights.

(The Authors)

STEVE W. J. KOZLOWSKI and DANIEL R. ILGEN study the dynamics of teams at Michigan State University.

Works Well with Others

Finally, whatever the task, the way people perform, or *do,* the work as a team makes a profound difference. The important elements here appear to be general teamwork skills that are not specific to any particular task. Some of the research in this area centers on bad behaviors that degrade team performance and spirit—dealing with "free riders," for example, who rely on other team members to do their job and thus contribute less than their fair share. This type of disruptive behavior can be limited by requiring that contributions be visible and members accountable.

There are also many positive ways in which the best teams act that give them an advantage: individuals are aware of one another's performance, provide backup coverage for members, set goals, coordinate their actions, communicate effectively, make decisions, resolve conflicts, and adapt to changing circumstances and new ideas. A key point is that this learning process can be a dynamic one that helps to shape and improve the team over time—and team leaders can play a major role. Prior to action, for example, the leader can help set team learning goals commensurate with current team capabilities. During action, the leader monitors team performance (and intervenes as necessary). As the team disengages from action, the leader diagnoses performance deficiencies and guides process feedback. This cycle repeats, and the complexity of learning goals increases incrementally as team skills accumulate and develop. This kind of feedback loop has been shown to reliably improve team thinking and performance.

Work from Kozlowski's group, however, has found a trade-off in the type of feedback provided and the resulting performance. Feedback directed to individuals yields higher individual performance at the expense of team performance; team feedback yields better team performance at the expense of individual performance. If both types of feedback are provided, both levels of performance cannot be maximized. The findings indicate that team designers need to be mindful of

On-the-job training: every task a team undertakes is a chance to learn new skills and to learn how to work together more effectively.

ASHLEY COOPER *Corbis*

precisely what they want to be salient to team members and should design supporting goal and feedback systems accordingly. Such systems may need to be adaptive, shifting the balance depending on current needs.

One reason that achieving the right level of feedback is so important is that teams learn best while doing. In some cases, notably in the military and in aviation, this on-the-job training can be supplemented with sophisticated and realistic simulations of combat missions or of takeoffs and landings. This virtual training approach is starting to find applications elsewhere, such as in medicine, although in most cases the best place to develop team skills is on the job itself. General teamwork proficiency turns out to be one area where classroom training appears to make a strong difference, perhaps because these are generic skills not related to a specific job. Accordingly, semester-long college-level programs that significantly improve students' knowledge of generic teamwork competencies have been developed. Nevertheless, encouraging work by one of our teams (Ilgen's) has demonstrated that knowledge of these team competencies can improve significantly with only 30 minutes of individual training.

Missed Opportunities

Although these skills can be taught, they rarely are—and few formal experiences to impart generic team-process and leadership experiences are available. If such courses are provided at all, they tend to be very late in the educational process—in college courses or in professional programs such as business school, for example—and these courses are usually geared toward imparting factual knowledge rather than building skills. We sampled a number of well-known M.B.A. programs and found that fewer than half listed a course devoted primarily to leadership or teams.

Furthermore, although it is not uncommon for educators from elementary school through college to include assignments organized around group projects in which students may display

teamwork and leadership behaviors, attention is usually on the group's output—a report, for example—with little or no attention placed on guiding the nature and effectiveness of the team process.

If teamwork were taught along with reading, writing and mathematics, and if these skills were ubiquitous, there would be enormous benefits to students and society alike. For now, though, it is often only after a great triumph or tragedy that the importance of teamwork is drawn into the spotlight. Ironically, these occasions focus largely on singling out individuals for reward or to assign blame, as the case may be. Despite literally thousands of studies that show much can be done to design teams properly and to ensure they do their jobs well and get better as time goes on, the question rarely turns to how the successes can be replicated or problems avoided the next time around. We think it is just a matter of applying the science. **M**

Leaders play a crucial role in developing group skills by setting goals, monitoring performance and giving feedback.

ERIN RYAN *zefa/Corbis*

(Further Reading)

◆ **A Multiple-Goal, Multilevel Model of Feedback Effects on the Regulation of Individual and Team Performance.** Richard P. DeShon, Steve W. J. Kozlowski, Aaron M. Schmidt, Karen A. Milner and Darin Wiechmann in *Journal of Applied Psychology,* Vol. 89, No. 6, pages 1035–1056; December 2004.

◆ **An Evaluation of Generic Teamwork Skills Training with Action Teams: Effects on Cognitive and Skill-based Outcomes.** Aleksander P. J. Ellis, Bradford S. Bell, Robert E. Ployhart, John R. Hollenbeck and Daniel R. Ilgen in *Personnel Psychology,* Vol. 58, No. 3, pages 641–672; Autumn 2005.

◆ **Enhancing the Effectiveness of Work Groups and Teams.** Steve W. J. Kozlowski and Daniel R. Ilgen in *Psychological Science in the Public Interest,* Vol. 7, No. 3, pages 77–124; December 2006.

Belief is powerful medicine, even if the treatment itself is a sham. New research shows placebos can also benefit patients who do not have faith in them

Cure in

By Maj-Britt Niemi

A man whom his doctors referred to as "Mr. Wright" was dying from cancer of the lymph nodes. Orange-size tumors had invaded his neck, groin, chest and abdomen, and his doctors had exhausted all available treatments. Nevertheless, Mr. Wright was confident that a new anticancer drug called Krebiozen would cure him, according to a 1957 report by psychologist Bruno Klopfer of the University of California, Los Angeles, entitled "Psychological Variables in Human Cancer."

Mr. Wright was bedridden and fighting for each breath when he received his first injection. But three days later he was cheerfully ambling around the unit, joking with the nurses. Mr. Wright's tumors had shrunk by half, and after 10 more days of treatment he was discharged from the hospital. And yet the other patients in the hospital who had received Krebiozen showed no improvement.

Over the next two months, however, Mr. Wright became troubled by press reports questioning the efficacy of Krebiozen and suffered a relapse. His doctors decided to lie to him: an improved, doubly effective version of the drug was due to arrive the next day, they told him. Mr. Wright was ecstatic. The doctors then gave him an injection that contained not one molecule of the drug—and he improved even more than he had the last time. Soon he walked out of the hospital symptom-free. He remained healthy until two months later, when, after reading reports that exposed Krebiozen as worthless, he died within days.

As Mr. Wright's experience illustrates, a patient's expectations and beliefs can greatly affect the course of an illness. When psychological factors tied to an inactive substance such as Krebiozen lead to recovery, doctors call the improvement a placebo effect.

In recent decades reports have confirmed the efficacy of such sham treat-

ANDY RYAN Getty *Images*

the Mind

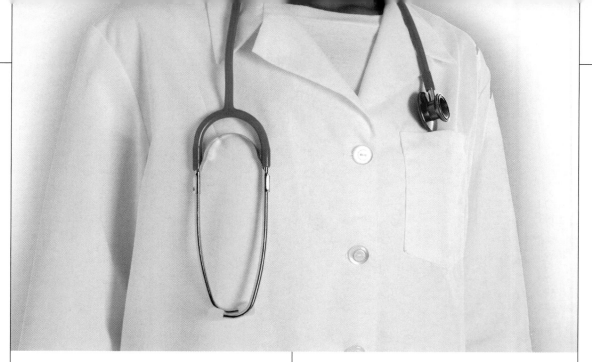

A white coat and a stethoscope can create a subconscious placebo reaction if a patient has previously associated them with feeling better.

ments in nearly all areas of medicine. Placebos can help not only to alleviate illnesses with an obvious psychological component, such as pain, depression and anxiety, but also to lessen the symptoms of Parkinson's disease and inflammatory disorders. Occasionally, as in Mr. Wright's case, placebos have shrunk tumors [*see box on opposite page*].

The latest research has shown that the placebo effect does not always arise from a conscious belief in a drug. Alternatively, it may grow out of subconscious associations between recovery and the experience of being treated, from the pinch of a shot to a doctor's white coat. Such subliminal conditioning can control bodily processes, including immune responses and the release of hormones. Meanwhile

researchers have decoded some of the biology of placebo responses, demonstrating that they stem from active processes in the brain.

Subconscious Cues

The placebo effect is probably as old as the healing professions themselves. In the 18th century physicians deliberately used inert pills when they had no suitable drug in their armamentarium. They spoke of supporting the healing process. After the middle of the 19th century medical scientists began viewing disease in purely physical and chemical terms. And by 1900 placebos had lost much of their previous popularity as therapy.

Indeed, modern medical investigators have often regarded the placebo response as a nuisance. But a cadre of psychologists, biologists, and other behavioral and social scientists instead view placebos as a key to understanding how the brain can control bodily processes to promote healing.

In the classic placebo effect, a person consciously believes that a substance is therapeutic, and this faith has a physiological consequence that dampens the pain or ameliorates other symptoms. Inversely, in the so-called nocebo effect, a negative attitude or expectation leads to harm or another undesirable outcome.

For several decades, however, researchers have known that placebo effects can also arise from subconscious associations as opposed to overt beliefs. Stimuli that a patient links with feeling better or with physical improvement—say, a doctor's white lab coat, a stethoscope or the smell of an examining room—may induce physiological reactions even if a patient has no explicit faith in the treatment being given. That is, simply seeing a doctor holding a sy-

FAST FACTS
Fake Fixes

1 ›› In recent decades reports have confirmed the efficacy of various sham treatments in nearly all areas of medicine. Placebos have helped alleviate pain, depression, anxiety, Parkinson's disease, inflammatory disorders and even cancer.

2 ›› Placebo effects can arise not only from a conscious belief in a drug but also from subconscious associations between recovery and the experience of being treated—from the pinch of a shot to a doctor's white coat. Such subliminal conditioning can control bodily processes of which we are unaware, such as immune responses and the release of hormones.

3 ›› Researchers have decoded some of the biology of placebo responses, demonstrating that they stem from active processes in the brain.

JUPITERIMAGES

BY GUSTAVO PACHECO-LOPEZ ET AL., IN *BRAIN, BEHAVIOR, AND IMMUNITY*, VOL. 20, NO. 5, SEPTEMBER 2006, AND "DOES A PLACEBO-EFFECT EXIST IN CLINICAL TRIALS ON MULTIPLE SCLEROSIS? REVIEW OF THE LITERATURE," BY L. LA MANTIA ET AL., IN *ITALIAN JOURNAL OF NEUROLOGICAL SCIENCES*, VOL. 17, NO. 2, APRIL 1996 (placebo chart)

Some scientists view placebos as a key to understanding how the brain can control bodily processes to promote faster healing.

ringe can produce a placebo reaction if a patient has previously associated that scenario with feeling better. In such cases, the overall effect—improvement or even complete recovery—stems from a combination of the pharmacological action of the drug and the subconscious or conditioned response.

My colleague, psychologist Manfred Schedlowski, and our team at the University of Duisburg-Essen in Germany and the Swiss Federal Institute of Technology Zurich have demonstrated that such conditioning can have pharmacological effects that mimic those of the drug being given—in this case, altering immune system status. We conditioned rats by first injecting them with the immunosuppressive drug cyclosporine A, which is used to prevent the rejection of transplanted organs. At the same time, we fed the rats water sweetened with saccharin.

The rats apparently associated the cyclosporine with the sweet drink so that, later, feeding them the drink alone weakened their immune systems, presumably because their brain sent messages to the immune system that partially shut it down. Because the rats cannot consciously believe the drink is therapeutic the way a human might, unconscious, associative learning must have depressed their immunity. These findings suggest that a placebo effect does not require that a person hope for or believe in a positive outcome.

Immune Therapy

Subsequent transplantation experiments published in the 1990s showed that such conditioning has clinical significance. Rats that received a sweet drink that previously had been paired with cyclosporine A survived with the transplanted hearts of another rat species (which the rats' immune system would have otherwise rejected) considerably longer than did nonconditioned control animals. In some of the conditioned rodents, the transplanted hearts beat for more than 100 days, which suggests their bodies had accepted the transplants. Some of this work also hinted at a mechanism for this effect: in response to behavioral conditioning, the nervous system inhibits the spleen from releasing molecules called cytokines that immune cells use to communicate with one another. Such dampened immunity thus enables the body to tolerate a foreign organ.

Immune conditioning with cyclosporine works in humans as well. In 2002 Schedlowski, psychologist Marion U. Goebel of the University of Duisburg-Essen and their colleagues reported giving 18 healthy men a cyclosporine A capsule four times over three days, along with a greenish strawberry milk shake that smelled of lavender. Not surprisingly, their immune systems showed signs of reduced function. Five days later, when the subjects took just a dummy capsule (but no active drug) with the strange drink, the beverage similarly weakened their immune system, though somewhat less than cyclosporine had. In contrast, no such effect was seen in 16 men who received a dummy pill throughout the experiment. "This study demonstrates for

Placebo Medicine

Disease	Average percentage of patients in whom placebo therapy worked	Number of studies; total number of participants
Cancer	2–7 (tumors reduced in size)	10; 464
Crohn's disease	19	32; 1,047
Chronic fatigue syndrome	19.6	29; 1,016
Duodenal ulcer	Healing in 36.2–44.2	79; 3,325
Irritable bowel syndrome	40	45; 3,193
Multiple sclerosis	11–50 (fewer episodes after two to three years)	6; 264

> Subliminal suggestions can manipulate involuntary physiological responses, such as hormone release, more than conscious beliefs can.

the first time in humans in a double-blind, placebo-controlled design that behavioral conditioning is able to mimic the immunological effects of an immunosuppressive drug," the authors wrote.

Subconscious placebo responses can also dampen the overactive immune responses that give rise to allergies. In 2008 Goebel and her colleagues reported conditioning 30 people who were allergic to dust mites by giving them, on five consecutive days, an unusual drink followed by a tablet of the allergy treatment desloratadine. This drug blocks the action of histamines, which mediate allergic reactions. Later, 11 of the patients received the novel drink, along with a placebo pill that looked like desloratadine, whereas the others received plain water and either a placebo or the drug.

The subjects who later sipped the strange beverage, but not those who drank water, showed a reduction in their allergy symptoms, accompanied by lowered immunological reactivity comparable to that seen in those who took the desloratadine in the second phase of the experiment. Thus, the placebo treatment measurably attenuated the subjects' immune response.

But what is the neurological basis for conditioned placebos? In a 2005 study Schedlowski and I, along with our colleagues, identified several areas of the brain that play a role in cyclosporine-saccharin conditioning in rats. We selectively damaged the brains of rats in each of three areas—the insular cortex, the amygdala and the ventromedial nucleus of the hypothalamus—before or after the rats underwent the first phase of conditioning in which they were exposed to cyclosporine paired with saccharin [*see box below*].

We found that the insular cortex—an area that modulates sensory experiences such as taste along with emotions and the physiological state of the body—is essential for conditioning at all times. Animals with a damaged insular cortex exhibited no conditioned immune response, no matter when

Training the Subconscious

A person can experience a placebo effect even if he or she has no explicit faith in a therapy. Subconscious conditioning can do the trick. During such conditioning, a person or animal inadvertently associates a stimulus, such as an injection, with a pharmacological consequence. In medical offices, this may happen, say, when a patient associates a doctor's white coat or syringe with feeling better. In research laboratories, investigators can deliberately condition animals to respond to an inert substance.

Such intentional conditioning involves two phases. In the first step, called the acquisition phase, an animal such as a rat receives an active drug—say, an immunosuppressant—over several consecutive days. Scientists call the drug the unconditioned stimulus. At the same time, the rat is given a neutral stimulus such as water sweetened with saccharin. This inert substance becomes a so-called conditioned stimulus by being paired with the drug.

In the second phase of conditioning, called evocation, the animal is given the inactive beverage without the drug, and the

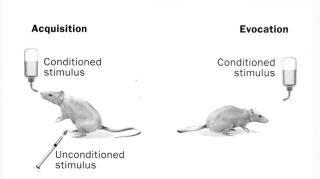

If rats receive an inactive beverage (the conditioned stimulus) along with a drug injection (the unconditioned stimulus), the drink alone may later produce an effect like that of the drug.

drink alone produces a pharmacological effect similar to that of the drug. In our experiments, the drink produces a weakened immune response. 　　　　　　　　　　　　　　—*M.-B.N.*

MUSTAFA DELIORMANLI iStockphoto (stethoscope); COURTESY OF MAJ-BRITT NIEMI (rat experiment)

Along with sub-conscious cues, dummy pills can dampen overactive immune responses and thereby thwart allergies.

the experimental lesion was made. Yet an intact amygdala, which is involved in emotional learning, was indispensable only for immune conditioning during the first, so-called acquisition phase of conditioning, suggesting that the amygdala governs the input of visceral information, including the status of the immune system, during learning. Lesions to the hypothalamus, in contrast, had an effect only if they were made after the initial acquisition phase of conditioning, indicating that this almond-size neural structure participates in relaying information from the brain to the immune system to evoke the conditioned response.

Expecting Relief

Given the power of conditioned placebo effects, scientists have wondered whether conditioning might account for most such phenomena, leaving only a minor role for expectation. Data suggest, however, that expectation does often contribute but that its influence extends mainly to symptoms that humans can perceive, such as pain.

In 2003 neuroscientist Fabrizio Benedetti of the University of Turin Medical School in Italy and his team tested the relative influence of expectation and conditioning in 60 volunteers who underwent a procedure that caused severe arm pain. They gave some of the participants a saline injection and told them the shot would intensify their pain; other volunteers were also given the placebo pain promoter but in addition underwent conditioning to decrease pain in which the saline shot was preceded by injections of the nonsteroidal anti-inflammatory drug (NSAID) ketorolac. In both groups pain increased, demonstrating that

negative expectation is a powerful nocebo in the case of pain. What is more, anticipating more pain led to increased agony despite conditioning to an analgesic, showing that expectation influences pain more than conditioning does.

On the other hand, suggestion is relatively impotent when it comes to involuntary bodily responses. In another experiment in the same study, Benedetti's team told participants that a saline shot would alter levels (either up or down, depending on the group) of growth hormone or the stress hormone cortisol. But the suggestions had no effect on either hormone. In contrast, a saline injection did alter hormone concentrations when the researchers conditioned subjects with sumatriptan, a drug that influences their secretion. These placebo-induced biological changes occurred even if the participants were told the saline injection would have an effect opposite to that of sumatriptan. Thus, conditioning can manipulate involuntary physiological processes more than conscious beliefs can.

Expectation and conditioning placebos also work through separate biological mechanisms. In an experiment conducted by Benedetti and Turin neuroscientist Martina Amanzio, volunteers who received a shot of saline touted to be a pain reliever could bear more pain in their arms than they could without the shot. No pain relief was evident, however, when the saline was replaced by naloxone, a

(The Author)

MAJ-BRITT NIEMI is a psychologist and researcher in the department of psychology and behavioral immunobiology at the Institute for Behavioral Sciences, Swiss Federal Institute of Technology Zurich.

JUPITERIMAGES

Dummy-Drug Doping?

Researchers have shown that placebos can activate the body's own painkilling opioids. In particular, saline injections can dampen pain if a person has recently received shots of morphine, a powerful analgesic, and has thereby associated such injections with pain relief. Could such a procedure be used to boost pain tolerance during athletic competitions?

According to the prohibited drugs list of the World Anti-Doping Agency, morphine is illegal during athletic competition but not during training. So an athlete might legally inject herself with morphine before competition, only to replace that injection with a placebo on the day of the event. To be effective, however, such a strategy requires that the morphine be taken several days before the placebo so that no trace of the drug would exist on competition day, and until recently, researchers were not sure whether the conditioned response would still be effective after an interval longer than a day or so.

In 2007 neuroscientist Fabrizio Benedetti of the University of Turin Medical School in Italy and his colleagues reported simulating a sports competition in which four teams of 10 young males competed with one another in a test of pain endurance. During the training, two of the teams were given morphine injections once a week for two weeks. Then, a week later, just before the pain tolerance test, members of one morphine-exposed team were injected with saline they thought was morphine. Indeed, that combination produced the greatest pain tolerance as compared with no injection, an injection of saline

New research suggests that athletes could use placebos to legally enhance their performance at competitive events such as track meets.

without previous exposure to morphine or a shot of an opioid-blocking drug.

These results show that only two shots of morphine, separated in time by as long as a week, are enough to induce a strong and long-lasting placebo response, which could significantly boost pain tolerance in an athlete on the day of a competition. Because an athlete who took morphine a week earlier is not likely to test positive for the drug, such a placebo procedure would be legal. But given the placebo's power, doping agency officials might start asking whether it should be.

—Ingrid Wickelgren, staff editor

substance that blocks the function of the body's natural painkillers, endogenous opioids. This result suggests that the expectation effect works through the release of these opioids.

Then researchers conditioned subjects by preceding a saline injection with doses of the NSAID ketorolac. But in this case, the resulting placebo effect was *not* blocked by naloxone. What is more, naloxone only abbreviated the placebo response from saline paired with ketorolac when the participants also believed that the saline was a pain-blocking agent. In other words, naloxone exclusively impinged on the conscious part of that pain-reducing response. The scientists conclude that the placebo effect can consist of two components: the expectation effect, which is mediated by opioids and abolished by naloxone, and the conditioned effect, which seems to work in the same manner as whatever analgesic is used in the conditioning—and is therefore not generally sensitive to naloxone.

Additional support for the notion that endogenous opioids are behind the expectation effect comes from psychiatrist Jon-Kar Zubieta and his co-workers at the University of Michigan at Ann Arbor. In 2005 the investigators reported using molecular imaging techniques to measure opioid-mediated neuronal activity in the brain while they induced sustained muscle pain in volunteers. During one of the scans, the investigators gave the volunteers a placebo infusion of plain saline that doctors described as a medication "thought to have analgesic effects." Compared with the trial in which no infusion was given, the saline produced increased activity precisely in those brain regions that inhibit pain and stress through endogenous opioid neurotransmission, the researchers found. In addition, the volunteers reported lower ratings of pain intensity in the saline-injection trial, suggesting that a placebo with expected painkilling properties relieves pain by acting on the brain's endogenous opioid system.

Along with a flurry of activity from brain opioids, placebo analgesia is also accompanied by a quieting of brain regions responsible for processing painful sensations. In a 2007 study neuroscientist Donald Price of the University of Florida and his colleagues used magnetic resonance imaging to scan the brains of patients with irritable bowel syndrome while they underwent a painful procedure. Price's team showed that when patients believed they were receiving an analgesic, not only did their pain diminish but neuronal activity also declined significantly in five pain-sensing brain regions as compared with trials in which they were not given a fake painkiller.

Placebo Performance

Despite the proved power of suggestion, investigators have been unable to identify personality traits that increase susceptibility to placebos. Personality, after all, has little effect on subconscious conditioning. For such subliminal responses, presentation matters more than personality does. Giving a medication a popular brand name or prescribing more frequent doses can boost the efficacy of a placebo. Similarly, a physician can maximize a placebo effect by radiating confidence or spending more time with the patient. Such tactics may subconsciously build a patient's trust in a therapy.

A high price tag on the drug can apparently help, too. In one study, placebos reported to cost $0.10 worked considerably less well in relieving pain than did those priced at $2.50 per pill. Test subjects evidently distrusted the less expensive medication. Patients are also liable to benefit more from placebos that involve elaborate medical procedures than from those requiring simple measures. Thus, the most effective sham treatments may extend beyond dispensing inactive pills to a simulation of a multistep therapeutic regimen.

As evidence of this idea, counseling psychologist Cynthia McRae of the University of Denver and her colleagues reported in 2004 the surprising success of a sham brain surgery in improving the quality of life of patients with advanced Parkinson's disease. Surgeons performed the sham operation to compare its efficacy with that of implanting human embryonic dopamine neurons into the brains of Parkinson's patients, who suffer from a lack of dopamine. In McRae's follow-up study, which assessed the patients' quality of life up to a year later, the researchers found that the patients who received the sham surgery were doing just as well physically, socially and emotionally as were the patients who had received the new cells. What mattered was not the transplant itself but whether a patient thought he or she had received it.

In recent years extensive research revealing the many medical applications, types and mechanisms of placebo effects has given credence to this once orphaned phenomenon. Doctors are now considering placebo pills and procedures as a way of enhancing the effectiveness of drugs and surgery. Such uses may elicit new controversies and questions such as the use of placebos to boost athletic performance [see box on opposite page]. In the meantime, sophisticated doctors might decide to manipulate the conscious and subconscious mind in ways that could cure—or at least, do no harm. M

> Giving a medication a well-known name, prescribing more frequent doses or indicating that it is expensive can boost the efficacy of a placebo.

(Further Reading)

◆ **Conscious Expectation and Unconscious Conditioning in Analgesic, Motor, and Hormonal Placebo/Nocebo Responses.** Fabrizio Benedetti et al. in *Journal of Neuroscience*, Vol. 23, No. 10, pages 4315–4323; May 15, 2003.

◆ **Neural Substrates for Behaviorally Conditioned Immunosuppression in the Rat.** Gustavo Pacheco-López et al. in *Journal of Neuroscience*, Vol. 25, No. 9, pages 2330–2337; March 2, 2005.

◆ **Placebo Effects Mediated by Endogenous Opioid Activity on μ-Opioid Receptors.** Jon-Kar Zubieta et al. in *Journal of Neuroscience*, Vol. 25, No. 34, pages 7754–7762; August 24, 2005.

◆ **Expectations and Associations That Heal: Immunomodulatory Placebo Effects and Its Neurobiology.** Gustavo Pacheco-López, Harald Engler, Maj-Britt Niemi and Manfred Schedlowski in *Brain, Behavior, and Immunity*, Vol. 20, No. 5, pages 430–446; September 2006.

◆ **Taste-Immunosuppression Engram: Reinforcement and Extinction.** Maj-Britt Niemi et al. in *Journal of Neuroimmunology*, Vol. 188, Nos. 1–2, pages 74–79; August 2007.

◆ **Commercial Features of Placebo and Therapeutic Efficacy.** Rebecca L. Waber, Baba Shiv, Ziv Carmon and Dan Ariely in *Journal of the American Medical Association*, Vol. 299, No. 9, pages 1016–1017; March 5, 2008.

◆ **Behavioral Conditioning of Antihistamine Effects in Patients with Allergic Rhinitis.** Marion U. Goebel et al. in *Psychotherapy and Psychosomatics*, Vol. 77, No. 4, pages 227–234; May 2008.

ISTOCKPHOTO

NOTES